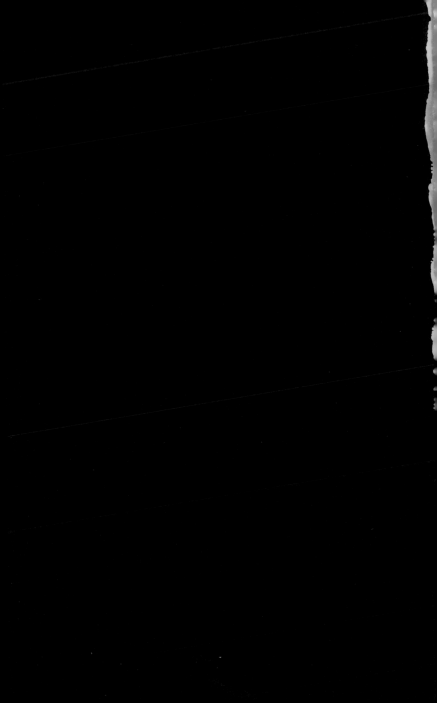

NOT HAMLET

Janet Suzman

Not Hamlet

*Meditations on the Frail Position
of Women in Drama*

OBERON BOOKS

LONDON

First published in 2012 by Oberon Books Ltd
521 Caledonian Road, London N7 9RH
Tel: +44 (0) 20 7607 3637 / Fax: +44 (0) 20 7607 3629
e-mail: info@oberonbooks.com
www.oberonbooks.com

Reprinted in 2012

A catalogue record for this book is available from the British Library.

HB ISBN: 978-1-84943-201-6
E ISBN: 978-1-84943-601-4

Printed, bound and converted
by CPI Group (UK) Ltd, Croydon, CR0 4YY.

Visit www.oberonbooks.com to read more about all our books and to
buy them. You will also find features, author interviews and news of
any author events, and you can sign up for e-newsletters so that you're
always first to hear about our new releases.

Contents

Acknowledgements

I HAVE PARTIALLY USED an interview reprinted from *Playing Joan: Actresses on the Challenge of Shaw's Saint Joan: Twenty-Six Interviews* by Holly Hill, published by Theatre Communications Group, 1987, used by permission. I have interwoven thoughts on La Pucelle, Shakespeare's Joan, which I played in Peter Hall's quatercentenary season of *The Wars of the Roses* which launched the Royal Shakespeare Company. To Peter Hall's brilliant pragmatism on the matter of verse, and to his inspired masterwork, the great cycle of seven history plays, I owe a huge debt of gratitude. I have long wished to say also that I have not known a better design to accommodate those histories, and I take this opportunity to salute the late John Bury: his mighty revolving periaktoi, sparking iron weaponry, gunked royal richness – his whole inspired Gothic steel-mesh war-world – sent scenes bowling along with a swiftness and economy never again to be emulated on a more cumbersome traverse stage.

In 1987, to celebrate the 150th anniversary of Ibsen's birth, I was invited by Prof. Erroll Durbach at The University of British Columbia, Vancouver, to deliver a paper on Hedda Gabler, amongst a most distinguished company

7

of Ibsenites. Amongst that scholarly array the only way to offer anything like an original viewpoint, it seemed to me, was to talk my way through the play's particularly dense dramatic underbrush as if in performance. I have used, with permission, most of this talk, but with alterations that render it both fresher and clearer on the page. I hope. And with a growing awareness that trying to describe performance is a fool's game. The papers from that conference were published in *Ibsen and the Theatre* by Macmillan and permission is granted. A far shorter essay on Hedda appears in *Blackwell's Companion to Twentieth Century Theatre*.

I have made comments on key moments in *Antony and Cleopatra* in notes to *The Applause Shakespeare Library*'s edition, edited by Barry Gaines, for which I wrote the textual commentary. However, I wish to further develop these into a cohesive argument for seeing Cleopatra as a far more interesting animal than is generally the case, and thereby also reassessing Antony's tragic pathway. To Trevor Nunn who started me off on this journey of giving the Egyptian Queen some wellie, my thanks, and I daresay that I am now the person in the world who knows her way around this play better than most having played it in both Stratford and London, filmed it for TV, and later directed it. Twice. Firstly at the Liverpool Playhouse in 2010, and then at the Chichester Festival Theatre in 2012. Both times with Kim Cattrall as Cleopatra. Antony was Jeffery Kissoon for Liverpool and then Michael Pennington. Irene Worth once confessed to me that the only regret in her professional life was not ever having played Cleopatra and that is our loss too.

It was the *Hamlet* I directed for the University of Cape Town's Baxter Theatre that suffered the fatal shock of losing its Guildenstern on Easter Sunday 2006 to a drugged and murderous pair of thugs. Brett Goldin, together with a friend of his, Richard Bloom, was abducted late on Saturday night and they were found shot the next day. Shot in cold blood, for no reason – for Hecuba. Brett was so excited by his first trip overseas, and so longing to be playing in Shakespeare's town. His Guildenstern was cheeky, vulnerable, troubled, and a lousy liar. Only *Hamlet* could have taken yet another death on board with such largesse, and allowed grieving room to its young cast while they valiantly continued to give the play the life Brett was denied. I am going to say here that I have not seen a pair of spies developing their individual differences so interestingly; those twinned eminences are usually indistinguishable one from t'other. That this bright spirit could not come with us to The Swan to open The Complete Works Festival at Stratford-upon-Avon, was tragic, albeit nothing to his mother's loss.

I find myself often being fascinated with the more peripheral parts in Shakespeare – though it has to be said Tom Stoppard already occupies this area uniquely – and whether this interest is because I am a woman and super-aware of underdoggery, I am not sure. Suffice it to say that having once played both, I would recommend Celia over Rosalind as a forest companion. But here at Elsinore, I found that the weird journeys of both Gertrude and Ophelia began to fascinate. Hence their inclusion.

Prologue

WE CAN LEGISLATE in the workplace, in newly forged constitutions of newly freed nations, on corporate boards, in schools and on ships at sea – wherever women need to be given a better chance to excel, but we can't do a damned thing about art. No legislation there other than not to curb it.

But as years roll on, you can't help noticing the unevenness of it all, and I don't think it is at all to do specifically with a woman's talent for playwriting, it's any talent male or female, and it just so happens that the most enduring roles for women have been written by men. There is an impressive scad of women playwrights hitting the boards with their work at present – a good round dozen at the last count – all of them prodigious, self-assured, brilliant and young. But like the Chinese man said about the French revolution, it is too early to tell. Tell what? Whether the work stands that old thing, the test of time.

It's high time that a young woman could say the following – it's Laura Wade who wrote *Posh* among other plays: *'…there's no reason why the work we produce shouldn't be any less epic or political or brutal or beautiful than the stuff male writers produce... We are coming into a world where the door is absolutely open.'*

I have high hopes – royal power being a thing of the past – that the domestic tragedy of a present-day Hedda will find in, say fifty years, it has lasted out the passing of fashions, fads, slang and popular faves-of-the-month to endure as the saga of an universal cross-cultural Everywoman. Or that a political leader, unlike poor Mrs Thatcher cast in amnesiac default mode so she won't seem too strong and frighten anyone, is given the full historical nation-changing treatment with nobs on. One of these young writers will have done that, impossible to say who, and still lots to come. But I bet what won't happen is a female dramatic character with a brain the size of Everest, a humour to match, and an unfolding story that has nothing to do with how she looks but only how she thinks and feels and reads the world.

Let's see. *La lutta continua...*

A Rogue Prologue
A heartfelt plea for a bit of common sense

A FRIEND OF LONG-STANDING, – I shall call her X in time-honoured fashion – suddenly declared her interest in the Earl of Oxford not that long ago. The Earl of Oxford? Who he? I knew only dimly that he'd been singled out by people who have nothing better to do than doubt Shakespeare's authorship of his own plays. Since everything about Shakespeare, his life and his genius, remains a profound mystery, the piling on of further obfuscations shot through with cant, piffle and deception seems to me a poor subject for deep analysis. Furthermore, to waste good millions on a lousy film to defend the indefensible seems both profligate and time-wasting. Even spending my time on this counter-blast is slightly irritating. But I find myself wanting to defend the man from Stratford here; the one person in the known universe who doesn't need my defence. But there you go, he's got it.

My friend had the grace to seem a little shame-faced, embarrassed even, as if confessing to some childhood misdemeanour. For my part I was unexpectedly shocked, as if a betrayal had occurred. Having fallen in love with

English long ago in a hot African schoolroom, I am honour bound to declare my fealty to the man from Stratford; his authorship of his own plays and poems makes perfect sense to me while blasting those same senses to smithereens. Still, paradox is the name of the Shakespearian game, is it not?

I knew this much about the time-wasters: that for many a decade Shakespeare's breathtaking talent and huge output has addled the brains of mere mortals, and so the easiest way out of addlement is to assign the entire canon to another, more conventionally educated, brain. Thus Francis Bacon was suggested as author, by a great-great-great grand niece of his called Delia Bacon in the late nineteenth century. No one up to then had bothered to smell a rat. Then Christopher Marlowe and Ben Jonson had their turn in the Imposters witness box, but since these candidates had several credibility flaws, like talent, style, and timelines, the poor hapless Earl of Oxford was finally appointed instead. Then a pair of rather grand American novelists took up the cause and, most worryingly, Sigmund Freud. A man whose language was not English but whose brain was amazed at the psychological accuracy of Shakespearian characters. To this day I know of a group of Freudian psychoanalysts who meet every third Sunday in Hampstead to study those dramatic motivations in detail from the playtexts.

The reasons for Oxford's latter-day coronation seem tenuous bar that he lived almost but not quite concurrently with William, wrote a few poems of uneven quality, had foreign adventures, was rich and well connected, was patron of a theatre company for a time, talked occasionally to Queen Elizabeth when he wasn't being banished by her, but chiefly possessed a suitable geography in his life, having travelled a fair amount both to the Continent and the Americas, as is the wont of young aristocrats. Oh, yes, and had a classical university education, learning his Latin and Greek at Oxbridge, which naturally makes him a genius. I joke.

Travel makes it possible, you see, to write plays set in foreign climes. For your Oxfordian, it's impossible for a writer to conjure up another world in the imagination, he has to have been there, which for a start puts the entire range of science fiction into the rubbish bin. I am not aware that Shakespeare ever offered up street maps of his towns, Rome, say, or Verona or Padua, though he did mention the Rialto, the incredibly famous Venetian bridge. I guess he'd heard of it like I had. But there you are, that's what Oxfordians require – topographical accuracy; the metaphor of the plays is quite beside the point to this lot. The notion that you can't write about anything until you have been-there-done-that is just silly.

As to X, I just could not understand why so sensible a person had embraced so cloudy a cause. Surely she was old enough and wise enough to know better than to espouse the suspicions of a bunch of conspiracy theorists, and worse still, snobs?

Because this is what it boils down to: you have to be a conspiracy theorist to imagine the Earl of Oxford secretly wrote thirty-seven plays performed and printed over a quarter of a century without being found out. Don't you? And you have to be a snob if you just hate it that the greatest poet the world has ever produced was born into the humble aldermanic classes of a provincial town. I'm not even querying that one.

So, not being a scholar or an academic, I hereby consider myself free to throw down a gauntlet unconstrained by the chivalry and accuracy of those noble professions. I'm a mere actor, I can rant all I like. And it is from the actor's standpoint only that I shall do so.

I guessed, I think rightly, that secrecy to the Oxfordians is the very drug that feeds the illusion; *'The thrill of a transgressive life'*, is how X had weirdly put it to me. Anyway, I have now done a little more research on these people's views but remain unimpressed by their dark constructs of lies and elaborate secrecy; so depressingly unShakespearian.

Still, I must forgive my old friend, though remaining puzzled. She pointed out that the Earl had penned some *Poesies* incognito, as aristos didn't like being published in the vulgar marketplace, hence their poetry was circulated privately amongst their noble acquaintance. The lines I subsequently read have no feel of Shakespeare's originality or largesse while remaining respectable enough. It is as well to be reminded that the modern idea of authorship, where you own every word you write and can be sued for borrowing a syllable of anyone else's, and where your entire reputation rests on public acknowledgement of your works under your sole name, is a fairly modern phenomenon. In Shakespeare's time collaboration was the order of the day, and it was only after the publication of his raunchy and beautiful 'Venus and Adonis' poem that the name of William Shakespeare became a useful selling point to his publisher.

In 2011 a murky and far-fetched film was released – Sony-backed, shame on them wasting their money on such a bad subject – called *Anonymous*; the invented story of how this poor put-upon Earl of Oxford was the real author of the plays. No facts to back it up, just wild submissions and some quite good cinematography of the gloomy historical documentary kind. Some months before seeing it, I had been invited to a debate before it went on release, where incidentally it received universal critical trouncings. Professor Stanley Wells, the Rev Dr. Paul Edmondson, and Professor Michael Dobson of The Shakespeare Institute and the University of Birmingham were present to defend William. To traduce William were present the director of the film, Roland Emmerich (bet they couldn't find a British director to do the hatchet job), a distant descendant of the Earl's, and a little man from a small but perfectly misguided suburban university which gives degrees in maligning Shakespeare – and whose name I have forgotten.

My impression of the affair was very much the experience proper scientists must have when attempting to debate with creationists. The only point I remember the director offering up was that Susannah, William's daughter, was unable to write. Well, Dad was keeping himself pretty busy in London for most of her childhood, and mother had no time in the day to teach the poor kid, trying her best to keep food and drink on the table. In reality Susanna's laziness is debatable, but we will never know for sure. Oh, yes, and the other point was the puzzling one about Shakespeare's papers and books not being mentioned in his will. Well, Will's Will is a subject for fascinating scholarly conjecture and there's no space for that here, but I expect Will had already taken good care of them, being ill and thoughtful for a long time before dying. I am glad to report that filling the room at the English-Speaking Union that evening were perfectly sensible people who know that Shakespeare wrote Shakespeare, and who showed some impatience at the daft lot who don't.

Roughly this is how their batty film version goes: Oxford was always secretly writing plays, having written *Midsummer Night's Dream* when he was about eight years old and henceforth entranced with his own prodigiousness, he continued in secret. But how was he to get these works into the playhouses without revealing his blue-blood? The Queen would have had him topped had she known. Thus Oxford, desperate for a theatrical conduit, singles out Ben Jonson, playwright, needing money for a reason I cannot now recall, and Ben is duly blackmailed and sworn to silence – a brilliant writer libelled beyond recognition.

Oxford could now feed his plays through Jonson's bribed hands to reach the actors. However, one day a doltish and illiterate member of the acting company – justify an illiterate actor to me please – namely one William Shakespeare, finds out about the deception and so poor Ben has to pay him clandestinely, courtesy of the rich earl, to keep his mouth shut. Oh, and for the use of his nice name. Thus it is that he, dim-witted Will, got all the kudos for the huge success of these plays. We should be thankful that comical Will Kempe wasn't chosen as the dupe in this film – a close call; consider the dull thud of The Royal Kempe Company.

Has it never occurred to this bunch of dreamers how such a daft plot might work in a busy theatre company? Their scenario only works off torture and bribery anyway. There wouldn't be enough money in the universe to stop all the actors in a company from blabbing till Doomsday, let alone the masses of other people involved in a theatre company; the tirers delivering head dresses, the sewing women mending torn costumes, the butchers and bakers and candlestick-makers. No whispers and sniggers about such a plonking modus operandi, a deception stretching over twenty-five years? Did this doltish William of theirs never crow in his cups about his secret benefactor and his growing wealth? Did the Company never notice how illiterate Will had suddenly turned scribe, brandishing inky cue-sheets under their noses, scribbly fingers freshly stained? Did no one ever mark how rewrites – for rewrites there surely were – happened only after this William returned from a loo-break? We must assume the author earl was in the building that day skulking about in the gods ready for consultation. You think the cleaning-woman didn't spot him as she swept up the vomit and hazelnut shells? A conspiracy, you understand, demands silence from everyone; unattainable in a theatre company, with skittering boys and prying eyes all on the loose in a

building with no doors to shut on secrets. If they d
blab they were inhuman, and actors are all human, t
for sure.

It becomes increasingly evident that the Oxfordian view
of human nature is just a touch – well, out of touch. What
do people do? They gossip. Universally, they gossip. To
this day and forever, they gossip. What makes Oxfordians
think human nature has changed? A mystery. When all is
said and done the reason why William Shakespeare's plays
remain as vibrant as ever is because human nature hasn't
changed; they tell us stories about recognisable human
beings. All of them with natures like ours, some the size
of giants, others our size, all of them recognisably us in
extremis. These guys have badly lost the plot.

Not to mention that the earl dies in 1604 and
Shakespeare lasts till 1616, but hey, no worries, the late
plays secretly mature in the company cellar like bottles of
vintage claret, to be broached one by one with a flourish
when a new play is required. In the silly film a pile of
the late plays are tremblingly handed by the dying earl to
Ben Jonson for safe-keeping. Ben then manages to hide
them in a tin trunk beneath the stage. For nine years those
plays lie safe, undiscovered by prying prop-hands. Then
the terrible Globe fire of 1613 happens, and lo! – they are
rescued by panic-stricken Ben. A sigh of relief when he
notes that *Antony and Cleopatra* is sooty but all there for

posterity. Well, whew! But this silliness hides a very serious point: if the Oxfordian bunch assume that the late plays could have been written early it beggars belief about their understanding of the maturing trajectory of not only this supreme mind, but any writer. It assumes a genius that not even a genius could have managed. *Oh, please...*! My italics show the extent of my impatience. I know I am not alone in this.

Here's Peter Brook in his essay *Alack Poor Yorick* writing vividly on this central question, the daily life of a busy theatre company, left entirely unaddressed by the Oxfordian illuminati:

> We must never lose touch with the communal nature of theatre... An actor says to an author – 'This bit seems a bit long, couldn't we cut it?' or 'I haven't enough time for a costume change – could you write a soliloquy or a little scene on the forestage to help?' Imagine a fake Shakespeare put on the spot?... No-one smelled a rat amongst all those spiteful and jealous rivals? Even today, imagine a phoney writer. The cast would begin to notice and gossip about the fact that every time you ask something, the author slips into the wings with his cell phone.

In case anybody is still under the illusion that a complicated thing like a play just happens without rehearsal here is an enlightening corroboration which I quote from Germaine Greer's *Shakespeare: A Very Short Introduction*:

> Elizabethan popular drama was unique in Europe in that the playwrights insisted on absolute control. In the introduction to his verse translation (1610) of Thomas Tomkis's morality play, *Lingua*, Johannes Rhenanus described how such control was exercised. 'So far as actors are concerned they, as I noticed in England, are daily instructed, as it were in a school, so that even the most eminent actors have to allow themselves to be instructed by the dramatists, which arrangement gives life and ornament to a well-written play, so that it is no wonder that the English players (I speak of the skilled ones) surpass and have the advantage of others'.

You only have to hear the funniest scenes in the canon written about actors playing actors in *The Dream* to realise the author was familiar with the ways of – er – actors. It's written with love, sympathy and mockery all tumbled in a whole heap of theatrical 'nous'. Oh no! – sorry, Lord Oxford wrote it when still a mere lad, I quite forgot…

Greer continues:

> Hamlet's speech to the players mirrors this… situation…and he gives precise instructions

in the manner of delivery, 'trippingly', not mouthing and grimacing or obscuring the matter with exaggerated gestures: 'let those that play your clowns speak no more than is set down for them'. (3.2.38-9)

A lot of ad-libbing must have gone on, there's a detectable rush of minor irritation at unruly actors. In the mouth of Hamlet Shakespeare is simply reminding actors given to coarseness, that over-acting is a bore. He suggests an unadorned style of delivery, speedy, full of clarity, and no unnecessary gestures. It holds good today, and is the most difficult to achieve. Less is eternally more.

No novelist (Mark Twain, Henry James) working alone, nor diviner of new pathways into the human psyche (Freud), nor scholar feeling his way through patterns of writing – ivory-towered and far from the marketplace – can know how a company of actors must resolve difficulties *fast and together*', again as Peter Brook describes the process. These three are the star names that hold to the Oxfordian view, and I am trying to think why. Freud was born into a poor family but it was a Jewish one so it struggled to ensure he was well educated. James was born into a rich one so he was OK. Twain made his adventurous way in the world after leaving school early, so he and Freud have a tenuously superficial commonality with Shakespeare's early life in the matter of relative poverty only.

Shakespeare's education at Stratford's grammar school – and it is far more likely than unlikely that he attended it – gave him a rigorous education in the classics and in rhetoric certainly well in advance of Twain's. Jonathan Bate comments that the level in these subjects reached when you left such a grammar school would be roughly equivalent to a first year at university now. There is evidence to show that other mercers of Stratford were well-educated and cultivated persons, and there is an extant letter written in Latin by a boy of eleven to his father, who was a friend of the Shakepeares (*The Essential Shakespeare* by John Dover Wilson). You could easily enough confuse Windsor with Stratford and come across Fords and Pages in either town with ease.

Conclusion? This illustrious trio's ignorance about how plays happen must be the deciding factor in their doubts about Stratford Shakespeare's abilities. No such excuse in the film in which a slew of brilliant actors, who surely know the process, take part. But the film is so laboured in the liberties it takes with known history that one cannot be surprised at its convolutions with unknown history. It proposes Queen Elizabeth had inside knowledge of the deception, had endless pregnancies and an away-with-the-fairies, *incredible* incestuous liaison with her own son (oh happy Freud!). Painting a woman of this worrying dimness and concupiscence is brought vividly off by the utterly brilliant Vanessa Redgrave whom we know likes embracing causes, though her presence in this snobbish film is a real puzzle. Still, such is my admiration for her luminous, unforgettable acting that I must allow her some slack. A stab at this disarmingly louse-ridden Elizabeth was obviously irresistible to her.

However, she is accompanied in the film by two other stunning actors, namely Derek Jacobi and Mark Rylance, where my leeway screeches to a halt. Both are declared Oxfordians. I keep wondering exactly when their own professional experience went flying out the window, and why? We have seen a dozen times how thrillingly they themselves can conjure up fantastical character studies of fictional persons – without ever having been crowned king or murdered a rival in real life? It's what actors do for heaven's sakes, and Shakespeare was one too. It's called imagination.

Theirs is a powerful gift that allows them to travel in the mind to any exotic land, to conjure up a brilliantly believable somebody, apparelled in clothes never worn in their own daily life, speaking in accents not native to them, comporting themselves in ways quite foreign to their own hearth, uttering thoughts way beyond any they themselves have ever conceived of. And these two great

Using imagination, don't need to 'be' or have experience of character

actors were born somewhere in the British Isles of parents as ordinary as schoolteachers and tobacconists, and yet they can do all this? It's called talent. And imagination is the central component of it. Rylance's naturalness with verse is supremely compelling, almost time-warping the listener into Hamlet's presence itself.

However William Shakespeare was not just clever but a rarer thing, a genius with a mind that no other being has come near to in the centuries that have unrolled since his time. Genius implies a huge capacity for concentration, for hard work, for long hours, for a voracious mind. He was a poet/actor, applying his sky-wide imagination to his trade in the company of just such fellows as Rylance and Jacobi. He wrote, they performed. As his flexibility with ideas and with verse matured, his colleagues must have been magicked by the power of his gift into ever more complex and responsive life onstage.

How strange then that Heminge and Condell felt moved to collate and publish the plays they had performed over the years, making a public tribute to their dead Friend. No hint or sniff there of the deception that the Oxfordians favour. The First Folio of 1623 is a loving tribute, righting the wrong of manuscripts previously *deformed by the frauds and stealthes of injurious impostors*. How strange it is that Jacobi and Rylance, hundreds of years later, with their outstanding acting instincts should embrace such a haughty view of the man who has made them as big as they are. I certainly don't advocate gratitude in them – though I often feel it – but common sense might not come amiss. With the respect due to both these very different actors, I shall continue to go on my merry anti-conspiracy way, trying to allow some sunlight through the murk of deception, while deference to their superior talents and confusion at their unaccountable amnesia about the process of playmaking continue to roil within me.

It seems to me that the entire history of the human race is the history of the immense struggle to move *upwards*; to overcome migration, to rise above bourgeois braces, to free oneself from the shackles of poverty, prejudice, and the Pale. Is it just my left-leaning propensities that recoil from the Oxfordian view that only an aristocrat can enter the soul of a king, or that only a university-trained mind can display such a ready wit? Goodness me, Shakespeare's Company gave nearly 100 performances before the courts of Elizabeth and James, did they think he was both blind and deaf? Or worse still, that an aristocratic mind is so unfathomable that a stranger to the class couldn't emulate its distinction? More interesting by miles than a man born into every privilege would be the creative anonymity of a most private man quietly observing London's throngs, the accents of strangers, the jargon of professionals, meeting people from all social classes and backgrounds – yes, *all*;

devouring books, poetry, plays, tracts, being as curious about everyone and everything as an artist should be in the excitement and turmoil of this greatest of river cities.

Here's Peter Brook again describing the exact same thing:

> ...We can imagine the young man from the country on his first days in London walking the bustling streets, sitting in the taverns and peering into brothels, his eyes and ears wide open, receiving impressions of travellers' tales, of rumours of palace intrigues, of religious quarrels, of elegant repartees and of violent obscenities. Given a unique avidity and power of receptivity, one single day or if you like, a week – could have given him more than enough material, social, political, intellectual, for a whole canon of plays. And in fact year after year he lived with this ocean of information feeding the unformed stories swirling around in his head. It is no wonder he was seen as a quiet man!

Charles Nicholl in his riveting book *The Lodger: Shakespeare on Silver Street* asks:

> Is there a note of escape in his removal to Silver Street? Is this rather quieter, more respectable, more anonymous neighbourhood something of

a bolt-hole from the boisterous and very public
world of players and playgoers?

He goes on to quote Aubrey's source, William
Beeston, as having remembered, or heard from his
father that Shakespeare *was the more to be admired*
[because] *he was not a company keeper. He wouldn't
be debauched, and if invited to, writt he was in pain.*
Writes Nicholl:

> This is unverifiable, but has the backing of
> common sense. It refers us to the reclusiveness
> of authorship, the staking out of mental space.
> Instead of partying...he will settle down to write,
> by candlelight, in the silence of the city at night.
> How else could his output – at least thirty-seven
> plays, two book-length narrative poems and
> 154 sonnets, not to mention his involvement
> in acting, directing, and general theatre
> management – have been achieved?

I have quoted at length from *The Lodger* because
common sense appears to be the only antidote to the
infuriating circumstantial woolliness of the Oxfordians
and thus provoked me into offering my penn'orth on
a subject already done to death. Nothing will quiet
their carping until a scrap of parchment comes to light
recounting an eye-witness account of Shakespeare at The
Globe actually writing on a cue-sheet and handing it

to Burbage or Davenant or Alleyn, standing foursquare on the stage of the Globe during a rehearsal, of let's say, *Othello* on a Thursday morning in 1604. Oh, and let's include in this fabled find a report of a debate between William and his actor about '*rich Indian*' or a '*rich Judean*' – which should it be? – to add an authenticating touch. All reported verbatim by our lucky witness. Dream on.

Failing that missing piece of paper we must rely on common sense and scholarship, since the Oxford bunch have chosen to ignore the plentiful direct and indirect allusions to the working writer, Shakespeare. For heaven's sake – we have at least a dozen known contemporaries of his who knew him well and who mention him both as author and actor; a continuous series of traces left from 1592 until his death in 1616. In the meantime Charles Nicholl's forensic investigation of where, when and how this quiet man could have been influenced by or have affected the people he knew and lived among is entrancing, scholastically deduced, and thoroughly believable. And the book is based on incontrovertible hard evidence: a court case in which William Shakespeare was a key witness.

How's this for a revealing clue? Antony to Cleopatra:

...and all alone tonight we'll wander through the streets and note the qualities of people...

That's what he did, I have no doubt, Will Shakespeare – strolled the streets of London, observing the life around him, invisible, unremarked, an ordinary man. It's tempting to think this fragmentary insight into his unreported life might be the sole piece of (whisper it) autobiography we dare infer from the entire canon.

After a youth spent in a cultural backwater, largely devoid of live theatre although very alive to the violence and avarice of living – Johannesburg – I can vouch for the joys of Learning Very Quickly once plunged into the magical maelstrom of London. I soon absorbed the fell gradations of the English class system, picked up the going lingo, met hundreds of foreigners, tried out my school French with them, and worse, my Cockney, generally adjusting seamlessly into ways that were strange to my upbringing. I'm no genius; it's the story of London.

Everyone is changed by it, and charged up by it. You expand your experience of human nature by leaps and by bounds, and chiefly, if you're an actor, you observe and you listen, you listen hard to the myriad accents around you; it's grist to your mill, it's your bread and butter. A modest demeanour and a Warwickshire accent, honestly come by, would have afforded a precious ordinariness to Shakespeare. The gentleness of his nature, mentioned repeatedly by admirers, would have drawn people out and his unforced interest would surely have invited conversation. He sounds like a charmer.

I'm guessing here, but just try to imagine the vigilance it would take for an earl to be amongst the vulgar, trying hard not to be recognised, adjusting his courtly accent, his refined manners, his entitled demeanour. I am assuming he had one, as this foreigner has noticed that the aristocracy can't help revealing its origins in casual encounter. I see him quelling his educated ripostes in an effort not to stand out, eager to hide some revealing gesture, tone of voice, haughty allusion which would inevitably give the game away in the stews and public houses. Even our friendly demotic Prince William is marked out by his perfectly ironed clothes. The Queen of Egypt and her lover strolling through the streets of Alexandria hoping not to be rumbled offer a sense of playfulness that is quite lacking in the relentlessly deceitful scenario of the Oxfordians.

Not only a dreadful snobbery pervades their view, but a limiting literalness that is hard to fathom, especially as some of their more famous adherents have perfectly respectable imaginations of their own. Why limit Shakespeare's jaw-dropping invention only to the louche accents of The Boar's Head Tavern or the bucolic sheepcotes of Arden just because the poor guy wasn't born with a silver spoon? Why can't he visit high battlements or a stormy beach on the coast of Illyria? Why not hot-headed Verona or ancient

Alexandria? You don't have to be Jewish to be Shylock or a prince to be Hamlet, so why should you be anything other than a writer to write? Nicholl again:

> It is a curious fact about the greatest playwright of Elizabethan and Jacobean England that not a single one of his thirty-seven canonical plays is set in Elizabethan or Jacobean England.

Is it not laughable to imply that a nobleman would have deeper insights into fatal love simply because he'd once passed through Verona on horseback?

My disappointment must therefore lie in my honourable but deluded friend somehow forgetting what an actor's life is like; how they don't suffer fools, how they can't keep a secret, how they have a nose for truth, and how highly policed a deception of this order would really have to be given all the perfectly solid, if brief, reports that sift back to us from Shakespeare's London.

James Shapiro, Jonathan Bate, Stanley Wells, Michael Dobson, Germaine Greer, Charles Nicholl, Samuel Schoenbaum, oh, and a thousand others, have done all that is academically necessary to clarify the differences then to now – the modern fashion for acknowledged authorship probably being the most germane. Germaine Greer offers up what she calls an *unassuming remark of Wittgenstein's which shows a way into Shakespeare's world*:

Shakespeare displays the dance of human passions, one might say. Hence he has to be objective; otherwise he would not so much display the dance of human passions, as talk about it. But he displays it to us in a dance, not naturalistically.

'By following this insight through its implications, we may begin to see how essential is Shakespeare's invisibility and how irrelevant his opinions', says Greer.

At the risk of repeating myself, it's understandable if non-theatre types get hold of the wrong end of the stick, but patience is stretched when people who know how plays are made get it so wrong. It's insulting to Shakespeare – that goes without saying – but it also insults those first-rate minds who have so profitably spent their time investigating the phenomenon.

Alexander Pope's Preface to the Works of Shakespeare 1725 might come as a timely reminder here:

Players are just such judges of what is right as Taylors are of what is graceful. And in this view it will be but fair to allow that most of our Author's faults are less to be ascribed to his wrong judgement as a Poet than to his right judgement as a Player.

In a straw poll put on the web by an Oxfordian-in-Chief the question goes thus: *'Is there any reasonable doubt that Shakespeare wrote the plays?'* – a blatantly leading question. Let's assume simply for the sake of argument there is a god, so if one were to pose the question: *'Is there any reasonable doubt that God made the world in six days?'* you might expect millions of people with half a brain to say *'yes there is a reasonable doubt because there is not a shred of hard evidence that He did'*. Holy Writ may be great poetry but it is not hard evidence. Thus it is reasonable to doubt. (I fully admit that bringing reason to bear on a matter of faith is contradictory, but still the query holds.) However, there are quite enough shreds of hard evidence that Shakespeare wrote lots of plays and equally that his contemporaries held him in both high and sometimes jealous esteem. So it follows that any 'doubts' must be *un*reasonable, and those doubts must depend on either incredulity or snobbishness, or both, but not on a lack of proof.

A fairer form the poll question might take is this: *'Do you doubt that a man without a university education could have written plays of that calibre?'* but that, my lords, has the nasty ring of elitism about it, doesn't it? So I daresay political correctness has got the better of the aristophiles? How paradoxical. A web-poll of those who stoop to ticking a box to malign a genius stands to shame his memory by depending, as everything does these days, not on the quality but the sheer dumbbell quantity of the box-tickers.

I have talked about the town, but even more central to Shakespeare is the country. I confess to being entranced with John Dover Wilson's small, deeply felt and expansive *The Essential Shakespeare*, expansive because he relates Shakespeare as a poet to another genius of the country, Wordsworth, and indeed to others like T.S. Eliot and Rupert Brooke. It's a captivating read for the likes of me.

> With most imaginative writers, memories of childhood and the natural scenes amid which they grew up are a primary source of later inspiration. It was so with Wordsworth; it was so with a very different writer, Dickens. It was certainly so with Shakespeare. His poems and early plays are as full of Warwickshire sights and sounds and characters as Wordsworth's poems are full of the Lake country. The influence seems to ebb as he develops, and then returns with redoubled force. And so, though we know nothing of his early life at Stratford, we can be certain of two things: first, that it made him a poet, and secondly, that it was the 'fountain light' of his poetic vision.

He goes on with his refreshing common sense to point out that Shakespeare must have been in Stratford nine months before the birth of Susanna, and was there to be married in November 1582; then again nine months before the birth of his twins – both conception dates are in the summer when the playhouses normally closed and it's presumed he would have returned home. Dover Wilson, sensible man, also remarks *'there is no ground whatever for imagining that his married life was an unhappy one, which is not the same thing as saying that he was a model husband.'* The plot of *Measure for Measure* hangs on Angelo's tyranny in condemning Claudio to death for marrying Juliet in just the fashion William married Ann.

I am going to continue for a moment longer with Dover Wilson's insightful comparison with Wordsworth as a country poet, by quoting these lines:

> *These beauteous forms*
> *Through a long absence, have not been to me*
> *As is a landscape to a blind man's eye:*
> *But oft, in lonely rooms, and 'mid the din*
> *Of towns and cities, I have owed to them,*
> *In hours of weariness sensations sweet,*
> *Felt in the blood and felt along the heart;*
> *And passing even into my purer mind,*
> *With tranquil restoration. ....*
> *While with an eye made quiet by the power*
> *Of harmony, and the deep power of joy,*
> *We see into the life of things.*

'*Wordsworth*', continues Dover Wilson, '*explains the last plays of Shakespeare, and the last plays lend to Wordsworth's lines the force of a new revelation*'.

We long again in age for the landscapes of our youth, and Shakespeare's return to Stratford cannot be surprising. Dirk Bogarde wrote: '*...you have to die in your own language*'. The importance of family always grows with increasing age unless catastrophe has struck your family life, and there are no hints of that, apart from the death of their young son Hamnet, a grief shared by William and Ann and made harder to bear by his absences, I feel sure. There must have been a lifetime of unfinished business with his wife and daughters. We feel the pull of the country growing in his plays; comparisons with the wit-slings of life at the court contrast with the sweaty freedoms of the country, the sheep-shearing scene in *The Winter's Tale*, *The Tempest* island full of sounds and sweet airs that give delight and hurt not. Greasy Joan is emerging again from his past to supplant that bad girl, Jane Nightwork.

If I had spent twenty-plus years churning out a canon of thirty-seven majestic plays for a demanding, creative, hard-headed acting company, in which each held shares so profits were a big deal, and business was competitive, and travelling exhausting, and entertainment a constant imperative, and threats of closure often imminent – sink or swim – I might also yearn to step back a bit as my fifties loomed and come home to my wife. A wife who no doubt had been project manager in situ on my large crumbling house, as wives always will. I would want to order my affairs and cultivate my garden and break bread with my family, and just...chill out. I would have been tired, and I would have earned the rest. He had. But had only four years left of life.

So, in the absence of the sort of hard evidence suggested above that would satisfy those who doubt the references to a living breathing writer called Shakespeare, I joyfully take recourse, not being myself a scholar, in the pragmatism of science to flag up my disdain for the conspiracy theorists. The profound linkage between art and science is magnificent: did not Einstein himself describe his theory of the universe as of 'incomparable beauty'?

The first principle belongs to forensic science, otherwise known as Locard's Exchange Principle that *every contact leaves traces*. That is the Principle that Charles Nicholl brilliantly makes use of for his book *Shakespeare on Silver Street*, triggering a minute examination *animated by a similar idea of proximity; of lives that touch, and the traces of evidence they leave... To find out more about the famous but so often obscure Mr Shakespeare, with whom they [the owners of the house where he lodged] were in casual daily contact*. His forensically examined essays in proximity, in clues and traces left in archives and court documents, in dialogue of his own and contemporary playwrights, by the people in Shakespeare's swathes of London, and his friends in Stratford [like Field the printer] is vastly entertaining. Even more telling, it smacks of the truth because it all seems so possible – more, eminently probable. Remember that not a single trace is discernible in the Oxfordian paper-chase. It's all smoke and snobbery.

And the second Principle I propose to invoke to swat away the baseless buzzing of the sceptics is known as Occam's Razor, meaning roughly 'simplest is best'.

I have sometimes invoked it for acting students when I teach – er – Shakespeare.

The following elegant explanation, for those of us who don't do science, I owe to my son, Josh, who is a physicist:

> The idea is that you always have a choice of different explanations [for a scientific observation]. Occam's Razor says you should choose the explanation that involves the smallest number of concepts or 'things'.
>
> Suppose you see a rainbow. There are an infinite number of ways to explain it. It could be that there's a leprechaun making the colours, but the leprechaun is invisible. It could be that on a rainy day there is a special substance in the air that makes colours when the sun hits it. Or, it could be that sunlight is composed of many

different colours, and raindrops in the air split them up.

The last one is the 'science' explanation because it satisfies Occam's Razor. It's the simplest explanation because it doesn't add any new concepts (like leprechauns or special substances), it just uses pre-existing concepts (light, the physics of refraction in water). Somehow it answers the original question (What makes a rainbow?) without simultaneously creating more questions (Where do leprechauns come from? Why can't I see them?)

I think it's interesting, because ultimately Occam's Razor is an *aesthetic* principle, which you can only really justify by saying that simpler theories are just 'more beautiful'. In some sense all of science can be viewed as a rather arbitrary attempt to satisfy this desire for beauty in simplicity. And if you don't sign up to the idea that simple is beautiful, well then you are quite justified in not signing up to science.

Well, there you go, I am signing up wholeheartedly to the idea that in science, in art, in life too, simplest is best. The poor Earl of Oxford's life, such as we know it, is way too complicated, not to mention too short, to have fitted into the sneaky diurnal disguise devised for him. Writing, directing, and acting in a slew of your own plays, in a company of performers who know you well, in a town abuzz with gossip and rivalry, for a quarter of a century is really more than enough for any one man to have accomplished. To have somehow *feigned* all this, god knows how, without being rumbled, simply beggars belief. And what about the collaborations, becoming increasingly clearer with closer analysis, with Middleton, Fletcher, and other dramatists of the age? Even the most eager Oxfordian could not write the scene where that happened. Occam's exquisite Razor leaps deliciously to hand to slash to shreds such barmy complications; Oxford did not write the plays. William Shakespeare of Stratford is the man who knows the quiet industry of creation and the hurly-burly of staging it. It's as simple as that. Otherwise we are truly away with the leprechauns.

Boy Actors

THE OTHER DAY I happened across Edith Sitwell's *A Notebook on William Shakespeare*, published in 1943, and this glorious sentence effulged off the opening page at me:

> Shakespeare is like the sun, that common-kissing Titan, having a passion for matter, pure and impure, an energy beyond good and evil, an immense benevolence creating without choice or preference, out of the need of giving birth to life.

Better that if you dare.

Professor Stanley Wells has no time for my unproven, and unprovable, contention that the boy actors of Shakespeare's theatres eventually turned into men actors. But with all respect for his by far superior knowledge of the period, I shall doggedly persist. Talent grows in direct proportion to the demands made on it. Let's suppose a youngster in Shakespeare's company had begun to prove himself with a heart-stopping Juliet, a smart stripling of a Portia or a lovelorn chatterbox of a Rosalind, and then moved on to, say, Imogen, Cressida or Kate, with growing flair, why say goodbye to such a boy once his voice breaks? Having learned so much in these younger parts, why not continue the journey when there are so many fine older female roles beckoning throughout the plays? Oh, of course, these parts didn't appear all at once, but as the years rolled by they mounted up, and surely it doesn't make much sense for an acting company to chuck away a blue chip asset?

Let's suppose that it was normal practice to use a child actor for small boy parts, and presumably a temporarily borrowed boy from the Children's Companies (Moth, Mamilius, Macduff junior, etc). Then if he showed promise get him back for the older girl parts (Hero, Bianca, Isabella, Portia), and now he's fully engaged to the acting company for young wife parts (Lady Percy, Hermione, Lady Anne), and queen parts (Isabel, Margaret of Anjou in Henry VI.i), and so on. However, the mad queens (that same Margaret seven plays further on), the strong-willed mothers (Volumnia, The Countess), the outspoken truth-tellers (Paulina, Emilia) need another story. And all this time the young boys are rapidly growing, their voices deepen, their stage technique widens, their life-baggage endows their characters with weight, and their personalities settle into a maturer skin? Then what? Give them their marching orders because they have a sprinkle of beard? Oh, surely not.

Does it not make perfect sense for young men who have done their apprenticeship to continue their careers?

Where's the profit in training people who have evident flair only to let them go when manhood kicks in? Shakespeare had a good business head on his shoulders. Why not assume that it was so very obvious a professional trajectory in the acting companies to nurture their specially gifted actors into adulthood that it didn't even warrant comment. Why write about the obvious? Am I wrong to assume we have no written mention of the practice because it was completely normal?

Englishmen, both straight and gay, have a rather endearing predilection for dressing up as females. The national cupboard groans to bursting with a bony host of psychosomatic reasons why this should be; exorcising their fears seems top guess. I'm not talking transvestism as it's psychologically a closed book to me, and anyway it's not a performance art, it's an addiction (I have read Grayson Perry's autobiography). Eddie Izzard might disagree. I simply mean the taking-off of old bags, your battleaxe stereotypes, for the sake of comedy alone, and the English do the poor old bags awfully well. Forgive me for saying English instead of British, but that seems to my eye where the talent lies. The Scots already have their skirts. Sometimes even the young battleaxes – what does one call them? – chavs? – are unnervingly recognisable, like the ghastly Vicky Pollard of *Little Britain* infamy. It seems a singularly English predilection to my eyes. I'm not sure that the Italians have taken to female impersonation with the same relish, or the French, Swedes, Germans, Scots, Canadians, Croats. (Oh, yes, one in South Africa.) To bolster its Anglo-Saxon DNA, there's a long pantomime dame tradition: that marvellous Shakespearian Ian McKellen had a ball doing his take on an Ugly Sister a few years back, greeted with euphoria as if doing a vulgar turn in a frock was the cherry on the cake of his Protean talent. This national taste for satirising females is primarily a camp romp, and the Ugly Sisters provide a time-honoured template for misogynistic humour, allowing quite nasty sexist jokes to be made, some of them genuinely hilarious.

The disguise gives the men the courage to speak their minds which may be something men as men never dare do? Is the idea behind it, I wonder, that women find greater moral courage in a corner than the male sex, and therefore don't need the disguise? Shakespeare certainly offers up loads of courage in his women, and what Shakespeare hasn't divined about human nature could be fitted into a cracked walnut. Remember Emilia dying for revealing the truth? Or young Desdemona defying social norms to marry her Othello, and roundly rejecting Emilia's exhortations to revenge, departing the stage for her deathbed with an unflinchingly brave couplet:

> *Good night, good night. God me such uses send,*
> *Not to pick bad from bad, but by bad mend.*

se are believable women; the point about male
s that they are not, in their comedic incarnations,
believable.

The cross-dressing tradition survives in a far more
sophisticated format than panto-dames as political and
social satire, and boasts two remarkably enduring creations
in Dame Edna Everage and Mrs Evita Bezuidenhout who
sprang, lurched more like, from the creative foreheads
of Barry Humphries and Pieter-Dirk Uys, to offer up
stringent comment on the age. Both men are tall, taller
still with heels, towering over their victims, and the
creatures they morph into are glitzily-dressed grotesques,
feigning a hollow modesty to parade their superior
wisdoms. Humphries keeps his humour personal, playing
into the ever-present obsessions with snobbery, class and
celebrity which beset this England. The smugly smiling
put-down is his stock in trade, and it adds to the gaiety
of the nation. Pity he's no longer gunning for the stars,
having announced his retirement; the nation will be duller
without his mischief.

Uys has a wider self-appointed remit, but only in the
context of South Africa, where history seems to have
found its usual depressing inclination to repeat itself, so
historical revisionism offers rich pickings to his sharp
eye. Yet having bided his time for quite a few years to
see how the newly liberated governance would shape up,

he has again come out shooting, and the present ANC government in its turn feels the sting of his mockery. Mrs Bezuidenhout has now manoeuvered herself away from the former character of Ambassador to the Independent Homeland of Baphetikosweti (an apartheid construct), away from the golden-hearted apologist for the crassest policies of the Nationalist Government, morphing into her current illustrious position of indispensable advisor-cum-nanny to Nelson Mandela, and enthusiast for all things black. Her grandchildren are black, a guarded grandmother's love surrounds their infancy, as she tells them bedtime stories in the dark.

Mandela himself loves Evita, being a man with an acute sense of humour, and so she was even invited to address the House of Assembly one fine day, although it's a rather trickier balancing act this time around to escape censure as a racist, he being white – 'the most famous white woman in Africa'. The irony is clear. He's drawn a deft acrostic comparison: Thabo as Botha, (ex-President Thabo Mbeki and ex-ex-President Botha), but Mr. Zuma's presidential voyage remains on course with more than enough corruption for Uys to mock for now, though there's a worrying new censorship law which badly holes the ship of state below the plimsoll line. Though it won't worry Uys. I have witnessed aldermen and town councillors of all colours practically curtseying as Mrs Bezuidenhout makes her grand way around an official welcoming cocktail party. A certain Free State town gave Mrs. B – so famous is she in SA – a civic reception, and reaching for a drink, the new black mayor accidentally brushed his hand across the Bezuidenhout bosom – bags of birdseed offer the right consistency – and a sweat broke out on his embarrassed forehead. These two supreme satirists seek shelter under the skirts of their alter egos, swathed in sequins and tulle, rather as Shakespeare's fools – Feste, Touchstone, Lear's fool, seek shelter from censure in their motley.

Nevertheless, stand-up and panto by grown-up hairy males is one thing but it's not theatre. They don't, can't, do real women with hearts and minds of their own. If I try hard I can sort of see Stanley Baxter broadly attempting a Nurse, a Duchess of York, a Merry Wife perhaps, and getting the laughs. I can't, however, see him touching your heart. It requires proper actors to give Shakespeare's rounded characters their due. Mark Rylance's mad-eyed wind-up doll of an Olivia remains a memorable take on a romantically self-dramatising young heiress, but it was more of a Rylance creation than Shakespeare's. Shakespeare always goes for humanity over type. I even remember Charles Kay and Ronald Pickup romping in the Forest as Celia and Rosalind, and that was good fun and finely tuned, but it wasn't Vanessa Redgrave's heartbreaking luminosity. How could it be? Ed Hall's marvellous Propeller Company, whose speciality is all-male Shakespeare productions, roar their way through the plays with both gusto and finesse, but these are not boys, they are grown guys, experienced actors, not whippersnappers with soprano voices.

The reverse is not true; women cannot play men, and it's a fairly hot-making experience to watch them trying. You can always add, you see, but you can't take away. Boys, yes, they can do boys – all the better if their shapes are androgynous enough – but not grown hairy men. After all, men's voices are more flexible if they're a tenor, reaching both lower and higher than their default, while women's voices simply can't go lower, so their range of octaves is limited, and their physical imitation of men ranges from approximate to pathetic. Although in a recent film called *Albert Nobbs* Janet McTeer brilliantly pulls off the part of a housepainter fellow, wondrously tall and rangy, spare with words, with self-confident amused eyes. In film the sentences are terse enough and the length of scenes short enough to get away with it by the skin of the teeth. The star of the film is Glenn Close playing a woman disguised as a butler, and I much admire her but I confess to feeling uneasy, her scrubbed little face markedly lacking a beard militated against total belief. Proportion has a lot to do with it; she looked delicate. I mean 'he'.

On the stage, where scenes are longer and deceptions more sustained, there's usually an important witness to the game hanging around, like Antonio the sea-captain, Celia, or Nerissa, and indeed you, the audience, the chief witness; all of us are expected to enter into the spirit of the game while thoroughly disbelieving it. Opera gets by because of the added magic of music and an audience happy to leave their judgement at home, but a play is not the place for stretching your suspension of disbelief too taut. You need to relax into a safe pair of hands. So a boy playing a young girl playing a boy is just fine – androgyny and innocence combine powerfully. A man with a light tenor voice playing a young woman is also fine, since tenor voices have more vocal colour at their disposal, both high and low, than a woman's voice can muster. (Anyway the best female voices have a lower register.) But come on! – for mature characters with gravitas, with wisdom, with a tragedy to unfold and a deep tale to tell, a boy's uninhabited voice will simply not do. I'm not buying it.

I remember an unforgettable performance of *Medea* given by Ninagawa's Japanese company, brought to the National Theatre by Thelma Holt in 1989. The most sinuous, obsessed, murderous Medea you could wish for, by the late Kabuki actor Tokusaburo Arashi, playing exquisitely what Sir Philip Sidney called *'the sour-sweetness of revenge'*. No added curves, the body of a supple man encased in an elegant sheath dress, disturbingly feline gestures, a flexible light tenor voice, and I understood at last the mystery of this ancient play, the incomprehensible mystery to a woman, of a woman who murders her children. The transformation achieved by Arashi into a mature female appeared effortless. It wasn't of course; the Japanese tradition has kept that as a special expertise, and this miraculous actor will have been trained in it from a small boy. As I write this, I understand that another great Kabuki actor named Hira (who originally performed in Ninagawa's production in Edinburgh before it came to London) is still giving his Medea in Japan, now aged 78. I swear Shakespeare will have had an actor or two of that order in his company else how on earth could he possibly write such richly fleshed-out roles for them?

Frankly I am amazed that scholars seem to accept the fait accompli of adolescent performers in these parts without further consideration. Hand on heart, I have heard grown men say in all seriousness that Cleopatra's line to Iras, *'And I shall see / Some squeaking Cleopatra boy my greatness / i' the posture of a whore'* as proof enough that boys played seriously complicated grown-ups like Cleopatra. Even when two lines later Shakespeare himself pooh-poohs that scenario by calling it *'absurd'*. Which it so patently is.

So I cannot be blamed for feeling a bit insulted, when adolescent boys are airily accepted as a given for the

Countess, for Paulina, for a raging Queen Margaret, for Volumnia, Constance, Gertrude – never mind the comic parts, Maria, Mistress Quickly, the Merry Wives, the Nurse. And what of Isabella, Hermione, Beatrice, Rosaline, Adriana? On and on goes the list of desperate, complex, outspoken, quick-witted creatures. But still, towering over them all, Cleopatra. Why would Shakespeare write those final two Acts, the climax to a long tale of ruined passion, if he wasn't damned sure that his actor could hold up, Atlas-like, not only Act V scene i where the queen reaches new heights, but also Act V scene ii – that last great scene – quite alone? Why would he unless he knew of an actor capable of being that Atlas?

So, the '...*boy my greatness*' argument is not quite refutation enough for me, I'm afraid, as the queen is envisaging the tumblers and clowns and low comedy boys doing the mocking – Caesar's *absurd intent* – in his Roman triumph. An Elizabethan audience would have envisaged Hamlet's annoying *'little eyases'*. To think a mere lad could get near to accomplishing those last two great acts of the play is beyond credibility, most especially as Shakespeare has his Cleopatra starting to speak verse as profound as grief, on an emotional level unlike anything that precedes the death of Antony.

The verse moves up to a higher plane on entering her monument, and once he has gone, Cleopatra reaches into

regions of herself as yet untouched. Her t\
dream of Antony is dreamed only after his death, i.
his failures still dogged their lives. And as to a young
laddie managing the jealous anger, the sexual come
the passionate exaggerations, the calculated flirting, the
theatrical hyperbole of the richly varied landscapes she
traverses preceding the final tragedy, no, sorry, it's too
patronising to bear. It will be a male academic that comes
pouncing after me I'll bet my bottom dollar, but I'll wager
not another self-respecting actress.

Let's face it, a performance of Antony and Cleopatra
with the company's resident heroic actor and this
presumed slip of a boy playing the queen must surely
have been a pretty lop-sided business back in the 1600s,
not exactly an equal pairing. Boo hiss. Shakespeare's
livelihood depended upon his audience being thoroughly
entertained, and it would have given short shrift, I'll bet
on it, to a mismatched attempt at these legendary heroic
figures. Imagine the mayhem if the groundlings weren't
convinced! A few school matinees of *Othello* at The Market
Theatre Johannesburg, gave me a pretty fair idea of what it
might have been like.

I understand there's no record of a contemporary
performance of *Antony and Cleopatra* but the bulk of it is
far too fabulous not to have been road-tested somewhere
sometime, probably at The Blackfriars where a limping

partnership would have piqued the patrons no end. Besides this legendary pair of mismatched lovers, how would the youths have coped with Hamlet and Gertrude in the closet scene? Beatrice and Benedick in the church? The Macbeths at home? Angela Pitt in *Shakespeare's Women* makes this point:

> Most of Shakespeare's plays were popular in his own lifetime. This was not because the audiences realised they were watching the works of a genius, but for the more down-to-earth reason that he captured their imaginations by showing them the personalities of their friends, their wives, their mistresses, their husbands and lovers, and themselves. The outward shape of Shakespeare's characters might well be that of kings and queens, and the plays themselves set in foreign lands, but the relationships and reactions evolved were totally comprehensible to the Elizabethan playgoer who might never have rubbed shoulders with the aristocracy nor been closer to the Continent than the south bank of the Thames.

I know perfectly well that you can scan the texts for anything you wish to prove and prove it to your own satisfaction, so rich are they in contradiction and antithesis, so broad in scope. It goes somewhat against the grain to highlight differences between the sexes in the long-drawn-out struggle for equality – and not over yet – when it has been vital to downplay the differences, but needs must. The chief wonder of Shakespeare is that nobody, but *nobody* can fathom him, so that those who say oh definitely, this is a gay writer, or this is unmistakably a misogynist writer can't prove a damned thing. They can huff and puff all they like and there's still masses of room left over for another somebody to aver oh, definitely he is heterosexual and loves women, or he's bisexual and loves them both equally – whatever. Shape-shifter: who he is, and how he stands, eludes us all.

And yet, and yet, he speaks for us all, whatever you want from him you can find. But without ducking and diving to prove this or that, I would say that the overwhelming ideal his comedies project is a wholesome coupling of man and woman, which, after all the trials the couple/s have overcome, is ideally compatible, cooperative, fecund, sexually vibrant, and above all, tried and tested in a frank mutual honesty. There is infinite room for doubt and darkness either side of this golden mean, but that's the constant. He is unmistakably Sweet Mr. Shakespeare.

There were women in his audiences (viz Rosalind's Epilogue), and those women were markedly more respected and freer than they had ever been before Elizabeth's reign, who nonetheless (shades of Mrs. Thatcher) made no effort to favour her female subjects. Still, during her long reign there was an indefinable spin-off due to her own remarkable qualities and that unique *'masculine power of application'* which her tutor Roger Ascham complimented her with.

And although Shakespeare wrote plays for some ten years into James's reign who was openly rather disdainful of women, alarmed by them probably, and who engendered an intolerance towards them, Shakespeare's vision of his women characters remains imbued with those Elizabethan qualities of assertive femininity.

As to the instruments that personify those energies: actresses today do not feel that they are only permitted onto his stage on sufferance. On the contrary, their presence bestows an effortless dimension of expressive femininity. Other perfectly familiar colours known to women seep into the rich warp and woof of his female characters, so it looks to me as if Shakespeare rather loves women since he writes them so awfully well. QED.

When Richard III mocks them for their sexual stupidity, he's not wrong; some women just do behave stupidly. You can divide womankind very roughly into Gertrudes and non-Gertrudes i.e. those who simply have to have a man to lean on else life is intolerable, and those who have learned to manage without dependency. The latter group is an ever-growing sisterhood in our time as economic empowerment weakens dependency, something little known in Shakespeare's day, thus forcing many a disenfranchised woman to sell themselves for a bit of bread. But certainly there were some women, his wife amongst them, who managed to manage without a man. Ann Shakespeare long outlived her husband, and most likely knew how to accomplish a full life.

I believe there are several learned essays on Shakespeare the misogynist, but I can't be bothered to read them, having played quite enough of his women to aver the contrary. Great actresses a generation above me, Peggy Ashcroft, Irene Worth, had no reservations about the extreme human warmth they naturally breathed into their performances, and two generations below me, the daughter of friends, writes to me yesterday: *'Just got cast as Titania…any thoughts?'* I shall quote her letter in full because it describes how completely Shakespeare's girls speak to a young American actress: *'I think this will be a good challenge for me because I'm so used to playing funny tomboy girls and Titania seems more like a steady, sultry warrior woman. It will be interesting to be in my body on stage that way. The language feels very different as well. Rosalind, Viola, Helena, and Kate all had a punchiness to them while Titania is very poetic and deep. At the same time, I wonder if she does have some funny moments or should I leave that all to Bottom?'* It only remains for me to reply to

Caroline to beg her not to try to be funny and the laughs will come. Otherwise she is spot on.

It is not difficult to mock people and write them off as the sorts of nags Shakespeare excoriates in *The Shrew*, and which the comedians plunder today, but it is quite another matter to write with respect of wives and women. And indeed to write with respect of marriage, and of which partner it is that usually works hard to keep a marriage going against all odds. Separation is always an enemy of matrimony, and I expect the Shakespeares' marriage had ups and downs, but given the outcome and ethos of the plays, it looks to me as if he thinks marriage, the *'world-without-end-bargain'*, is worth it.

There is, in many of his female characters such a kind of proud spirit and plain decency that one can't help suspecting that his wife, Ann, from whom he was absent for most of their married life, had a good dose of these virtues herself. Just maybe it was this silent soul in all her secret self-sufficiency, who might have been indirectly responsible for us having such a happily prolific Shakespeare? Happily for us, and one hopes also for him. There's a wonderful passage in the posthumous *Discoveries* of Ben Jonson, in which he famously praises Shakespeare: *'For a good poet's made as well as born / And such wert thou...'* It goes:

> When he hath set himself to writing, he
> would join night to day, not minding it till
> he fainted...he knew not how to dispose his
> own abilities or husband them, he was of that
> immoderate power against himself.

No wonder he was careful not to be drawn into all the drink and debauchery on his doorstep; he had plays to present and players to occupy and money to make, and seats to fill, and his concentration must have been superhuman.

So, there he was busy like a bee, scribbling away in London in his various lodgings, while she, Ann, a three days' ride away in Stratford, busily brought up their children. If dissent is assumed between them, there is no sign of it in his fictional world. If provincial puritan Stratford disapproved of the life theatrical, they might have changed their minds when they witnessed rambling New Place purchased by the absent writer, and its restoration project-managed by the wife, readied for his retirement. He must have sent money home regularly, with his sharp business brain, while the one that exceeds understanding went on beavering away in London. Well, who else would have fixed the place up if not her? It's what wives do.

Unlike some of his co-sharers in the King's Men, he was assiduous in conserving his growing wealth. One assumes he was usually present to oversee the performance of his plays, since stage directions are few and far between, but there's an unusually specific stage direction in *Coriolanus*: '*After holding her by the hand, silent.*' That's got to be an absent playwright making sure the moment between mother and son, so vivid in his head, is observed by the actors. I believe we know that he was in Stratford when the play was performed, dealing with a – possibly illicit – hoard of grain during the wheat famine of 1608. So, yes, the play's the thing and is obsessive, and just maybe Ann might have understood him. But that's another story. Germaine Greer has written on it and I found her take on their marriage in *Shakespeare's Wife* completely fascinating. Those who condescend to thinking this is just women's solidarity had better pull something better out of their hats than merely mocking a thesis simply because it hasn't been mooted before. Motives and proofs are lacking all around, but thinking yourself into the mindset of the age in such a thoroughly scholarly and detailed way raises haunting probabilities.

So, from the mystery of a particular and private woman to our public ones: a boy's uncomplicated treble in Shakespeare's extended speeches which ask for richer vocal colour. A low voice is, he finds, '*an excellent thing in woman*'. Don't we all? A man's voice could provide that. His mature characters express a greater range of emotion than an undeveloped youth can possibly find. Instinct may be a great matter, it might even be the greatest matter when addressing that unteachable talent that some performers possess, able to cut to the quick of a character. Emotional growth, however, comes at its own sweet pace. Caroline's development seems classic to me; she has matured into Titania. John Barton, to whom I owe so much, asserts that text *is* character. Yes, it is; if you find what's written for you, the character bodies forth, sucked out of no airy thumb. Imbedded in that dense text lie hidden all sorts of lovely clues as to character, stage business, and directions for getting on and offstage. Shakespeare is always an actor's writer. You learn to look for those clues by using your head. In using their heads, as the characters do, the heart is directly engaged. These two are indivisible components.

You scan the verse for clues, your mental radar a-bleep: where a caesura occurs and what it denotes, what a line of monosyllables does? Same query with polysyllabic words, and how thought and intention are affected by these pulses? Alliteration, assonance, conceit, image, metaphor, antithesis, end-stops, feet – a glorious list of structural clues for the mansions that Will builds. And then, having sussed out what use this knowledge might serve, you are clear to forget all about it and push open the great door duly armed with an emotional map clearly marked out. Now you won't lose your way on the journey to the bellowing minotaur within. If all this sounds a bit melodramatic, to Shakespeare's actors all these literary devices would have become second nature; the players not daunted by the task ahead of them. But in our picture-driven time the structure of how the poet uses the language to achieve what he needs is altogether fuzzier. We are less word-conscious, our vocabularies meaner and less wild.

Thought/emotion. Heart/intellect. A marrying of heart and mind that is uniquely his; as if we enter a Fourth Dimension when acting in his plays. Shakespeare is a super-realist, playing larger-than-life games with reality; his characters live on the verge of an abyss, courting imminent disaster, seeking life-changing adventures, playing with death and murder, dicing with undying love, demanding utter fidelity; they move on the black piste of fictional existence. I just won't believe that only boys had the pleasure of exploring these abyssal characters, rather than mature adult actors with bagfuls of life experience.

Forgive me, but I just have to quote again from the glorious effulgences of Edith Sitwell:

> Sometimes, amid the Titanic dust, the Titanic heat, a strange figure is thrown, that of the ancestor of Ancient Pistol and the Capitano of Italian Comedy. This shadow has drifted down the ages to us, escaped from the campaigns of Alexander, – retaining still his bluster, his tragic bombast, and with his tremendous

crest of plumes...still erect on his helmet. This being turns towards us, and we see, under the crest of feathers that is the mark of the soldier of fortune, a stock mask of Comedy, with empty eyes and open mouth – and, through these apertures, gain a glimpse of the face of Aeschylus.

In times of turmoil you can be sure that the face of Aeschylus, of Sophocles, of Euripides and of William Shakespeare, needs to be glimpsed, as we search for comment tumultuous enough for the world we live in. It interests me that Shakespeare is proving so very useful in prisons. Bruce Wall's London Shakespeare Workout has for many years been enticing prisoners into expressing themselves full out by means of Shakespeare's rule-breaking characters. Shake hands with Macbeth and you shake hands with a murderer, but a murderer who contemplates his deeds. I recall taking a verse class with a group in Pentonville Prison, under Bruce's aegis, and was fascinated by a huge black guy who chose Gertrude's speech when she observantly watches Ophelia drown. You don't ask what these offenders are inside for, but it did make me wonder. This man didn't make any attempt to become a woman, but the situation had spoken to him and he wanted to tell us the story in someone else's words. If Gertrude were invited to be a witness in a court of law she would be considered a good one, so forensically accurately does she recall the time, the place, the action, and the wildflowers. But in a court of law she might well be considered an accessory to a suicide not having lifted a finger to save a young girl from death. One of the other offenders chose Macbeth's insane vision of a dagger floating before his eyes. He spoke with such a matter-of-fact understanding of the speech, saying afterwards: *'Well, of course you don't want to admit that's your dagger, do ya? You'd get nicked for that.'* Such things spoken by fictional characters in full-blown verse, offering justifications and insights inexpressible to the speakers themselves, is empowering; it gives voice to their unspoken fears and undeclared motives. It allows them to acknowledge out loud acts of darkness in a form of heightened language that answers their needs.

What of the increasingly naturalistic interpolations of the later plays, and the emotionally expansive yet finely detailed performances they ask for? How could you expect to get that speed and flexibility from the truculent honesty that issues, uninflected, from the mouth of an adolescent performer? However talented, a boy cannot speak with conviction, let alone understanding: *'I have given suck and know what 'tis...'* et seq when there's palpably no way of his ever knowing. An adult actor might have had a wife in mind to help flesh out the image at the very least.

There is yet another possibility, far-fetched for the time given that women were kept under every known thumb, bar the Queen, whose Great Thumb ruled your life. Women actors. There'd be a watertight reason for the acting company to keep that intriguing possibility under the very strictest wraps for fear of the Puritan police rampaging in to arrest the lot of them. What fun to have a small coterie of intrepid Denchs and Paltrows stashed away in Clerkenwell and Blackfriars, primed and ready for the odd perf, slipping out of their digs dressed as boys, darting through the shadows, hooded and cloaked, to the stage-door of The Globe. This intriguing scenario is so much more of an incentive for a bunch of actors, to have a tee-hee Group Secret to keep under wraps, than the deceitful Oxfordian myth. The notion that flesh and blood women might have had the chance to play some of Shakespeare's younger women before their sudden vivid arrival onstage post-Restoration is not unique, and I know that Trevor Nunn for one is rather keen on the possibility. Again it's all conjecture, but has the smack of pragmatism about it, as well as acknowledging the sort of thinking on your feet and improvisational flexibility that to this day marks out the nature of a theatre company. In the entertainment maelstrom of London's Bankside Liberty, it's a distinct possibility.

At the court of King James there were many shenanigans, one of which is a hilarious report of a royal command performance by Sir John Harrington – a member of the Bedford / Essex / Sidney / Herbert group – describing the goings-on during the visit of Queen Anne's brother Christian IV in the summer of 1606, quite possibly the most alcoholic Royal occasion ever, outside of Blackadder's antics: '... *The entertainment and show went forward, and most of the presenters went backward, or fell down, wine did so occupy their upper chambers*'. He goes on to describe the fate of Hope Faith and Charity: '*Hope did assay to speak, but wine rendered her endeavours so feeble that she withdrew: ... Faith was then all alone...and left the court in a staggering condition. Charity came to the King's feet, and seemed to cover the multitude of her sins her sisters had committed...*' Admittedly these weren't exactly actresses, but the notion of females, courtiers or others, performing in some guise or other, was abroad.

Disguise is such a favourite theme in the plays, such a rich vein to mine that Shakespeare visits it often. How well he understands the heart fervently longing to escape from its hiding place into the clarity of an open and fair existence. '*I can live no longer by thinking!*' cries his Rosalind, and the relief that floods through the audience that revelation is at hand, is palpable. Rosalind has so much to say, so naturally and volubly do her feelings tumble from her mouth, that in truth only youth and fervency, no matter in what body these abide, matters. But what an added frisson there'd be if these were actually played by forbidden girls: Viola now a valiant valet calling upon her soul within the house, Celia admonishing her cousin for fainting at the sight of blood, Beatrice wishing herself a man so as to be taken seriously, as Cleopatra does too, later donning armour as *'president of my country'*, to *'appear there for a man'*, and La Pucelle, the most famous young girl soldier of all time.

Tom Stoppard's wonderful screenplay of *Shakespeare in Love*, proposes that there were girls with the same daft ambitions to be actresses as there are now and always have been. Women have been banned from the fun since memory began, but there's always a few rogue ones about, people with a dare in their hearts, prepared to take a risk. Do we imagine that way back then they didn't hold auditions for the acting company? (Shakespeare himself might have tagged onto a company of visiting players come to Stratford by just such a trial.) Do we imagine that occasionally there wasn't a bit of the old casting-couch hanky-panky going on? What makes us think anything has changed in the behaviour of chaps faced with the heady power of giving a girl a chance? Or a boy for that matter – but that is from our commission here. There's enough bawdy talk in the plays to let us know that our

Author was no slouch in the matter: viz the racy William the Conqueror anecdote, well attested. My secret favourite amongst the low-life characters jostling in Shakepeare's stews has got to be Jane Nightwork named fondly in that ravishing exchange of memory between Justice Shallow and Silence in *Henry IV*, an old girl gone to seed who once gave life a kick up the wazoo.

Don't let's assume the plays were just thrown on by an uncaring bunch of 'thesps', keen only on full houses and shared profits, and mugging up their lines at the last minute, like weekly rep actors doing their overworked best. Actors can be cynical but not about their art, their craft. Practice and rehearsals, discussions and arguments, adjustments, edits and additions would have gone on every day and far into the night most like. You can't half do plays, like you can't be sort of pregnant – it's all or nothing. That we have in common as professionals. And while there is so much of everyday existence in Shakespeare's theatres and his London that we can't easily envisage (compulsory church attendance on Sundays, the Spanish threat, the Star Chamber, an absolute monarch, the spies, the heads on spikes, the filth…) yet we should also seek out the common parts of our lives then and now. Take a bunch of modern actors reading Hamlet's advice to the players and it appears to coincide very well with our thoughts on acting today, so it looks like players then and players now see pretty much eye to eye on style and delivery. As to economy of expression, and an uncluttered taste, our confrères then appear to have much more in common with us than the wild and whirling rhetoricians of the Masham theatres where size matters.

It is the supreme achievement of Stanislavski that he had the common sense to codify a method of getting a role together that good actors will have instinctively done anyway. That being the case it might not be too far-fetched to infer that Shakespeare's increasing naturalism both reflects and predicts the fashion of his times for a style less rhetorical and grandiose than previously. The indoor Blackfriars would have encouraged such thinking probably. The Player King in *Hamlet* does a neat conflation of fashions passing in offering up a grand old piece of formal verse-speaking to a prince who is himself a master of the new style: 'Look', says Shakespeare, like a Picasso mischievously dashing off ten sketches of a bull each more economically drawn than the last, 'just look what I can do if I want to! Look how I can both mock and honour the old style in a breath!'

The most obvious things are not often recorded, just because they *are* so obvious, and so, as I've said, I do not doubt that adult male actors played the adult women characters. To deduce anything else would appear to relegate Shakespeare to being a dreamer rather than a practitioner. His plays are written to be acted. Actors are actors are actors, and no human behaviour falls outside their remit. Nor would I be surprised if several rogue and daring women played the younger female parts every so often when the coast was clear, surprising and bamboozling the audiences on various Globe afternoons. I prefer to part company with those critics and scholars who remain cocksure that boys were sufficiently good at the job to flesh out all of Shakespeare's women, merely because there's no written mention of an alternative. Common sense and the sheer quality of the writing belies that. Unless the critical faculties of an audience on Bankside were utter pants...

Cleopatra

I T'S THE RICHEST, most varied, most misunderstood part that Shakespeare wrote, and it's quite impossible to get it all. A woman with imagination and life experience of all kinds has a decent chance of getting most of it. A mature male actor with years behind him of playing female roles? Let's say a good half of it. A boy actor with none of the above, bar a certain flair, a vague grasp of how the other half thinks, a sharp eye, and who is lucky to have an elder sister or better still a temperamental mother, might have had a fraction of a chance. Else he should just opt for saying the words loud and clear, introduce a pout here, a flounce there, and pray that the audience ekes out the rest of this superhuman human with their imaginations. So one does rather wonder who Shakespeare had in mind when he wrote it?

If I am inclined to imagine that Shakespeare had some Dark Lady in his thoughts, and just possibly in his acting company from time to time, for the reason that his Cleopatra above all parts is quite beyond the sweet ignorance of a youth, it is because reports of women as far back as the 1600's are nil. Or are they? Here's the traveller Thomas Coryat, who from Venice in 1608 writes that he

'…saw women acte, a thing that I never saw before, *though I have heard that it hath been sometimes used in London*, and they performed it with as good grace, action, gesture and whatsoever convenient for a player, as ever I saw any masculine actor…' (My italics).

There's no record of a performance of this play, but performed somewhere sometime it must have been, most probably road-tested at The Blackfriars. It is rambling and populous, with about thirty-seven speaking parts, more scenes than *Hamlet*, and sporting the size and glamour, the restless movement of a big, big beautiful movie. And there's the rub, because a big big beautiful movie was once made of this story, with two big big beautiful stars involved in a real-life love affair, and such is the power of pictures that we still think of this play as a fatal love story, as if a mature and raunchy *Romeo and Juliet*, but it isn't that. The film was à la Cecil B. DeMille; it was called *Cleopatra* with every frame of it given the full Hollywood treatment, and the two stars were Elizabeth Taylor and Richard Burton, whose beauty and fame were legendary at the time, and still leave a residue of old-fashioned glamour hard to equal. Their real-life love affair got almost more publicity as it unfolded during the shooting of the film than the mighty story of the Queen of Egypt herself.

Physical beauty is so very rare a gift that when people possess it in abundance, as film stars sometimes do, we are bewitched. The gorgeousness of these two actors somehow imbued the historical characters they were portraying with the same attributes, which is a transference not entirely useful to our understanding of Shakespeare's play; for one, their glamour precludes our ever matching them. But there are other alternatives open to humbler beings, latter-day actors I mean; we can delve more deeply, understand the characters more profoundly, in a word, reveal more of their feelings than their flesh. That is what I prefer to attempt here. For really, *Antony and Cleopatra* by William Shakespeare is the tragic story of a once mighty hero obsessed by the Queen of Egypt, an obsession so fatal that it drags him to his doom. In that sense, it is, I venture to say, a male version of Phaedra. Phaedra conceived an obsessive passion for her stepson, which she was unable to conquer, and died for it. A woman's disease, this fatal love thing, you might say, but I am proposing it as a male one. This won't be well received amongst the scholastic classes but nevertheless, I shall hold to it.

Cleopatra herself is a far more arresting character historically than Elizabeth Taylor's fatally seductive cleavage allowed us to notice. In actual fact Cleopatra might not even have been beautiful, though blessed with spirit and intelligence in abundance. There's apparently a marble pillar with a bas-relief reputedly of her, though unverified, stashed away in the basement of The British Museum and a friend of mine, an Egyptologist who has seen it, says she strongly resembles Barbra Streisand. Several coins attest to a Streisand nose. Brainy women are too scary for most men to find sexy, though conversely slews of women just love brainy men. Ergo she must have been *une jolie laide* – trust the French to find a feminine grace that isn't vulgar – and thus enraptured both Julius Caesar and Mark Antony. It is unlikely and unproven that she had any further affairs. We do know she had an extraordinary voice, reported by Plutarch from many sources contemporary with her. He also attests to her *'irresistible charm'* and to the *'persuasion of her discourse'*. So there you are; she must have been quite something.

Actresses like to look for substance in the woman we are to play, at least I do, since an inventively flirtatious vocabulary is not fascinating enough an attribute to expend all that time and trouble on. It, the flirty thing, appears however to offer more than sufficient allure to the interested male, as when I have dipped occasionally into critical comment on this play I sigh at the predictably narrow parameters meted out to Cleopatra, reflecting I guess, a general opinion of women viewed from the manly groves of academe. *'Feminine wiles'*, *'deliberate unpredictability'*, *'conscious manipulation'* are much-used to describe her strategy to keep Antony fascinated. *'If you find him sad / Say I am dancing; if in mirth, report / That I am sudden sick'* (I.iii) is read as proof of her manipulative armoury, when in truth she's furious, and wants very much to disturb Antony. If I use the word 'truth' in relation to this fiction, I am of course referring to dramatic truth, whatever that may be. There is, I believe, a double standard in critical circles about judging the dramatic trajectories of male and of female characters. This is probably not even a particularly male habit, as very often women are harsh judges of women's behaviour too. All I wish to highlight is that Cleopatra's life and political judgements on behalf of Egypt are just as fascinating as Antony's from the Roman side. Being westerners, to this very day still at odds with the east, finding it both as loathsome and attractive as it ever was to the ancient Romans, the play retains a vivid resonance in our world where imperial powers still occupy lands once won and lost by Alexander the Great. It was a general of Alexander's army, Ptolemaeus from Macedonia, who was given Egypt as a reward, and his offspring is our very own Cleopatra VII of Egypt, who brought her beloved country to its knees in 30 BC. Brought to its knees because her lover, Antony, the Triumvir of the Roman empire, loved her too much, and lost.

I have to assume, or hope, that the reader will have the play by their side if anything I have to say excites an interest. It is, let's be frank, one of the most wonderful plays ever written. Worth the effort.

At the very start of the play, the moment *'News, my good lord, from Rome'* is dropped like a time bomb into an indolent Alexandrian court, all hell breaks loose. A story about an angry wife, a battle she initiates, and a whole heap of political tumult starts to unfold, and the mere mistress, queen-goddess of the Nile though she be, feels threatened. The idyll is at an end; that's how this love story begins. Real politik intrudes from the start.

The chief thing in playing Cleopatra is to know when she is acting up a storm and when she is telling a simple truth, and the rarity of the latter moments makes them even more astonishing, for those who have ears to hear. Act I scene iii is the most difficult scene between the lovers because of the dangerous way she handles the shock of his wife's death. The dishonesty of their relationship, their *'mouth-made vows'* unsanctioned by marriage (Shakespeare is the arch-eulogiser of marriage), piques Cleopatra into goading him almost beyond endurance, prodding the open wound of his adultery, mocking his dubious Roman honour, questioning his love and loyalty.

Fulvia, the absent wife, a constant threat to Cleopatra's safety, is ever-present between them, but hey! – when he displays no sorrow at her sudden death, she leaps, as it were, to the defence of Fulvia, thereby defending all wronged womankind (cf. Emilia's defense of wives in *Othello*). What a turn! She derides what Antony, all Romans, hold most dear, honour. That hits home! She affects to be the director of his drama, as if all his feelings are feigned, and rejoices in giving him bad-acting notes. The knife twists on 'say', 'play', 'look like'. She revels in his rage because at least it seems real:

> *Look, prithee Charmian*
> *How this Herculean Roman does become*
> *The carriage of his chafe.*

To retain any dignity in this onslaught of mockery, he must leave and with an angry

> *I'll leave you, lady*

– all politeness dropped – he stalks off. An ironic

> *Courteous lord, one word*

stops him. He must *want* to be stopped. Everyone knows that walking out in the middle of a row because you just can't cope, is bad, bad, bad. Yet the faint twang of irony on the word *'courteous'* covers her panic lest he go before she's had her say.

I bump up against a difficulty here in mentioning irony, a tone of voice which is impossible to convey on paper. I have to mention it, though, since it's a way of defusing incendiary behaviour which Cleopatra resorts to, sometimes to lighten the seriousness of a situation, sometimes to be funny. I sympathise with a critic sitting at a desk trying to interpret the dramatic intention of dialogue, but lacking the fine-tuned ear for changes of mood and tone without the presence of actors. (I read with surprise a critical comment assuming that Cleopatra truly means to abase herself to Octavius when she calls him *'My master and my lord'* in the final act. Well, no, actually, there is an extravagant mockery in the salutation which even my trying to define only succeeds in vulgarising.)

But I return to the longest and most knife-edge of all the scenes between the lovers: Act I scene iii. Having interrupted him repeatedly, made him more and more angry by teasing him unendurably for his dishonesty, her forces are now concentrated for their final onslaught. Her chilling quietness has made him turn, still wary – what now? 'Their entire story in one word?', he wonders. She's got his attention, so she offers two attempts at the simple truth expressed with a Petrarchan formality:

> *Sir, you and I must part – but that's not it.*
> *Sir, you and I have loved – but there's not it.*
> *That you know well.*

And just as you hope for peace between them, the caesura affords her space for a wicked U-turn:

> *Something it is I would –*

'Would what?' – would go on to say her heart is still as it once was, all his? But…but, right at this juncture when his 'Roman thoughts' have so expediently kicked aside their world like a squashed beer can, she feels 'to hell with it, I shall pretend to forget what we once were, just as Antony has already forgotten me':

> *O, my oblivion is a very Antony,*
> *And I am all forgotten!*

Cleopatra is not about to let sentiment cloud her deepest feelings; she feels sidelined, fragile, she feels her throne rocking, Egypt mocked. She will taunt, tease, mock, challenge, but never plead or kneel. That is the temper of that U-turn.

In case there are doubters about this reading, you have only to look at Antony's furious reply to her, amounting to this: 'If fools were not your subjects I would take you for the queen of fools'. It is always useful to look at a character's riposte to a speech if there's any doubt about the intention preceding it.

An angry man feeling like a fool himself? But no, she's not finished yet; you will not find another character in the canon who pushes the envelope so daringly. Once again, she speaks simply and truly, revealing her soul for an enticing four lines:

> *But sir, forgive me;*
> *Since my becomings kill me when they do not*
> *Eye well to you.*

To admit her *'becomings'* – histrionics – shame her if Antony can't see through them to her own pain, is to invite Antony's forgiveness, but that would be too easy. Rome

is just asking for more trouble from Egypt – Enobarbus
the great observer knows all about *that*. Another wicked
caesura provides the hairpin bend:

Your honour calls you hence;

What subtle tone invests *'honour'* with a faint tarnish,
while sounding in awe of it?

Therefore be deaf to my unpitied folly,

Mocking her silly little self before twisting the knife
further with a grand adieu:

And all the gods go with you!

Now another twist disguised as a formalised farewell
speech in the Roman manner:

Upon your sword
Sit laurel victory and smooth success
Be strewed before your feet!'

The repeated assonance gives a nice hiss of derision, and a
mildly sardonic bow to the laureate will rub salt into the
wound nicely.

For a further clue to the teasing tone of her speech, look
at Antony's curt:

Let us go.

No sooner said than regretted: in that instant he can't bear
to leave her so coldly, and his warm heart intervenes as he
turns back:

Come.

She, like him, at last lost in feeling, runs into his arms. It's a hard-earned embrace and puts an audience on its mettle with anxiety; quarrelling shelved under the stark stare of separation. His final speech, three lines of intense intimacy whispered into her ear, makes up for all that has gone before. Knife-edge stuff. And a last view of the lovers together for a very long time.

(This hard-won coming together will be ghosted in the terrible aftermath of the battle of Actium (III.xii) when one tear from her *'...rates / All that is won and lost.'*) If the actress tries to be charming in this parting scene, if she doesn't play it nudging the very brink of danger in the queen's emotions, if she doesn't fulfil to the letter Enobarbus's sensationally accurate judgement of her temperament, the two of them will miss the extreme sport of the play: the pain of separation.

Lest you think that her reaction to the tumult caused by Fulvia in Parthia, and young Pompey at sea is out of proportion, consider this: an abandoned wife is now dead, and unlamented. Antony's sworn adoration for his royal mistress might be just as hollow, and as it turns out it is. His marriage to Octavia attests. Meanwhile he has also idly ignored Cleopatra's back yard – *'all the east'* was his to govern. In a word, he has gone native and let their entire world go hang. Suddenly, this very morning, he must instantly leave to fix his shattered standing in the world.

Would you trust such a man? We know 'stuff happens', but in drama as in life it's not going to be an easy ride. However, if you find yourself defending Antony's return to politics, don't dismiss Cleopatra's later attempts at saving Egypt either.

I see in most criticism a patronising belittling of Cleopatra's provocations, the time-honoured armoury for all lovers, so that it is tempting to say 'guys, don't bother your pretty little heads with Shakespeare then', who is full to bursting with passion's strategies. The pull of opposites is drama's job, and antithesis its middle name. Mozart too: *'vorrei e non vorrei'* ('I want to and I don't want to' all sung in the same breath) is *the* essential dramatic dilemma. Both these geniuses thoroughly relish the feminine way of dealing with life's little revenges.

I also see a rather lopsided concentration on the role of Antony from male critics, who are accustomed, I suppose, to the man being the centre of any dramatic universe and are thus disabled from seeing what an amazing wood-for-the-trees-thing Shakespeare has done here; she is no longer just an adjunct, instead she is made the essence of the dramatic problem. I admit that this could pose a difficulty to an actor playing Antony, because actors are always, but always, rather used to having their own super-charged way in a play. An Antony, though, must find a paradox: the sheer magnitude of failure. He must permit himself to become enthralled, and think of it not as a weakness but as the very essence of the man. This Herculean Roman appears in a previous play, *Julius Caesar*, as his mighty soldierly self, but in this one he is the memory of that hero. Antony is unbearably moving in this play if his vulnerability and impulsiveness are allowed free reign. Never mind, an actor has plenty of other parts to soothe the savage ego. For poor underparted actresses, however, this part is unique in its range, size and independence.

Since Shakespeare's time, things have moved on a bit for us women, although when I look at the variety of roles he wrote for them I'm inclined to think the sheer length of Elizabeth's reign helped encourage a notion that clever women could also be considered as remarkable dramatic beings. There is nothing patronising in Shakespeare's attitude to the intelligence of his women. Beatrice is no fool, Volumnia's arguments to her stubborn son unimpeachably logical, Cleopatra a glorious mixture of everything. There isn't a Hamlet in a skirt, for sure, but there isn't another Hamlet in trousers either. Our archaeological sciences are better, so the period is better researched, though Plutarch provided Shakespeare with all he needed. Stacy Schiff's recent study, *Cleopatra*, is a mine of information on Cleopatra's period not available to Shakespeare, and it's a thesis that takes the queen of Egypt seriously for once. I am pleased to note many of my own instinctive feelings, based on the play itself, borne out in her thoroughly scholarly book. Does hard knowledge matter when acting this role? Not really, but it makes life more interesting for an actress to be able to pack some facts away for general use, as often verified fact is a useful bolster to a dramatic idea.

What intrigues me as I scour the play is the opacity of her true feelings for Antony, far more cryptic and elusive than Antony's feelings for her. The love affair is not an equal one, and his struggle to break free terrible: *'I must from this enchanting queen break off'* or *'Would I had never seen her!'* or *'And though I make this marriage for my peace, / i' the East my pleasure lies.'* These confessions to the audience bare a heart desperate to free itself from the thrall he is in. The struggle of the two Antonys has begun. Even a simple soldier on guard at the eve of the battle attests to Antony's Laocoön struggle with himself in one of the most haunting images in the play. The guard hears strange music from the air or from under the earth, and they wonder where it comes from:

> *'Tis the god Hercules, whom Antony loved,*
> *Now leaves him.*

says one of them. And in the very next scene, as he leaves his beloved on the morning of the battle, *'a man of steel'* – Cleopatra's sadness at his diminishment is palpable:

> *He goes forth gallantly. That he and Caesar might*

> *Determine this great war in single fight!*
> *Then Antony – but now – Well, on.*

His brain stops working properly it seems, so fatally does he proceed to misjudge events as they unfold: Cleopatra's mettle, his own enthrallment to her, his battle strategies, his own botched death; he even gets the name wrong of the officer Cleopatra should trust in Caesar's camp. With his dying breath he names Proculeis, but it is Dolabella she should trust.

The best clues to the protagonist's true state of mind are in the tiniest asides.

Her pride is badly hit by his shocking marriage to Caesar's sister, received as a personal insult, and the violence of her jealousy matches the hurt. It is a universal truth that the moment another woman enters the picture the lover becomes infinitely more desirable. Arguably more dangerous than a scorned woman is a wobbly throne, and hers has become unsafe without him: he must instantly be lured back into her sights once more. The fate of Egypt itself is at stake. In the midst of her raging fury at a poor messenger, Shakespeare opens a magic casement into Cleopatra's better nature. A sudden moment of self-awareness lends Cleopatra size and substance in this brief soliloquy:

> *These hands do lack nobility that they strike*
> *A meaner than myself, since I myself*

Have given myself the cause. (II.v)

At the end of this turbulent scene, here's a prime Mozartian moment:

Let him forever go! – Let him not, Charmian,

and oh, the pain in that. Then a burst of anguished curiosity about Octavia's looks, her age, her nature, her hair colour. Then the pain again:

Pity me Charmian but do not speak to me.
Lead me to my chamber.

There was a millionaire who used to boast that his car, a London taxi, *'could turn on a sixpence – whatever that may be'.* Cleopatra turns on sixpences so expertly you can hardly keep up with her; that's a great device to keep an audience on its toes.

To reiterate: the fabled love affair is on the rocks as the play begins; Philo's opening speech sets the scene:

Take but good note, and you shall see in him
The triple pillar of the world transformed
Into a strumpet's fool. Behold and see.

We behold and we see the legendary lovers exchanging challenging strophes on the depth of their love – a public display that has no basis in deeper reality. Easy-going, arrogant, unstinting in his adulation of her, yet Antony sounds just a trifle morning-after-the-night-before-ish, as he later disarmingly confesses to Octavius:

Three kings I had newly feasted and did want

Of what I was i' the morning.

He sobers up sharpish when the shock of his wife's death brings home to him Fulvia's great qualities:

She's good being gone.

(That will happen again at the end of the play, this time to Cleopatra, and engender a far more profound realisation of what is lost.) But right now the struggle to free himself from his *Egyptian fetters* has begun, a struggle doomed to fail, like a heroin addict going cold-turkey, so off and on is his resolve, so vulnerable his heart. She is more concerned with a discernable loss of power – out of sight, out of control – exacerbated by a blazing natural jealousy, which makes for great comedy. She rages, he suffers. That will change.

How paradoxical that the queen-goddess Cleopatra, theocratic supreme ruler of all Egypt, mother of his children, should feel herself reduced to a mere mistress, secondary to the wife. It's not all that easy to understand in these more equal days. But it is the queen, not the mistress, who is enraged at his absence, leaving her throne unprotected:

> *That Herod's head*
> *I'll have! But how, when Antony is gone*
> *Through whom I might command it?*

Shakespeare leaves us in no doubt that here is a functioning, if frustrated, monarch. Just before she interrogates the messenger who can report first-hand on Octavia, this mini-soliloquy of Cleopatra's reveals what's really preying on her mind.

Less power, more empty days to kill. She could fill them with unpeopling Egypt if she had a mind to it, such is her absolute power, but the fun is gone and enemies lurk. He must be *'nodded'* back. Those empty days provoke three delicious scenes of hyperbolic comedy. Don't be fooled into believing her every word, she is painting an amusing picture for her devoted audience – Charmian and the retinue – of a gloriously randy affair, as one does, playing up to the hilt a picture of an abandoned and heart-sore queen. It's all to do with inactivity, the lassitude of loneliness. I have a theory that all the great female love stories rely for their energy on passionate inactivity. We all know perfectly well that if you think too much you suffer. Everybody needs something to do. Work, as my friend Barney used to say, is the only dignity. (Think of Hedda's dreadful daily ennui while everyone else is busy knitting little garments or writing learned tomes; of *course* she's going to make trouble without her horses for distraction and adventure.)

Notice how, in his absence, all her memories of Antony describe him as he once was, not as he is now. The comedy in Cleopatra's time-filling scenes derives from her deliberate idealisation of Antony, amusingly dramatised, as playmate, lover, horseman, hero, sweetly avoiding his present tottering status. That is a theme throughout the play; Philo's opening speech paints a vivid picture of a military hard man lost to lust. Octavius Caesar's lament for his boyhood hero invokes Antony's former military glories to underline his present despised reputation. Even Cleopatra's great dream in Act V scene ii, is a quasi-mythical aggrandisement nostalgically infused with a thousand regrets.

I don't see Cleopatra as unaware of her lover's decline, but as unsure how to deal with it. His visibly diminishing skills elicit a veiled comment from her in III.viii more revealing, and more cryptic, than any other about what she thinks of Antony: *'That head, my lord.'* (III.xiii) says she. His soothsayer is newly returned from a request for clemency from a victorious Caesar, and tells him that the queen should yield up Antony in return for future negotiation. He bitterly proffers his head to Cleopatra:

> *To the boy Caesar send this grizzled head,*
> *And he will fill thy wishes to the brim*
> *With principalities.*

And her reply?

> *That head, my lord?*

That head is clearly no longer working as it should, *that head* has lost its mojo. I had an agree-to-differ conversation with the great Dame Peggy Ashcroft on this very line, which only shows what endless interpretations Shakespeare offers up. She considered those four brief words the shortest love poem in the language, expressing all that Cleopatra could not about her love for Antony.

I take the opposite view. I don't feel in all honesty this difficult moment in the action of the play is the time for a declaration of love, however brief. In this scene there is something restless, troubled, guilty, thoughtful, going on; much plotting and planning is swirling in the royal mind about the future of her children and her kingdom. This is what gives this play a dimension mightier than just a tragic love story. To my mind, the attitude invested in *'That head, my lord'* is the crucial clue to Cleopatra's inner life, and will serve as a touchstone for the actress in assessing Cleopatra's journey.

That doesn't mean she can't caress that *'grizzled head'* of Antony's, smooth it, embrace it, but her eyes above it, abstracted with thought, will tell another story. Antony doesn't notice her regretful insight; *'that head'* is far too busy avenging an humiliating defeat. She sits quietly, as if pensively observing a car-crash, silenced for once. She has silences, this queen, and they are always deeply felt.

The choice you make as an actor for a line as revealing as this, and as cryptic, since it gives nothing away, very much depends on how you assess Cleopatra's chances in relation to Antony after his defeat at Actium. Her power-base has been diminished, and so she, as queen, has to devise strategies cleverer than Antony's. That is why we see her building a relationship with Antony's closest friend, Enobarbus, valuing his straight talk. And now carefully taking the political temperature with Thidias, Caesar's messenger, in this very scene. She artfully wrong-foots the arrogant young officer, Octavius' emissary, Thidias, with a disarming *'What's your name?'* and then charms the socks off him, blatantly hinting at future concord with Octavius. When she holds out her *'blue-veined'* hand for him to kiss and is idly reminded of Caesar's attentions there, it is no mere nostalgic reverie but a deliberate ploy to impress. We are moving onto the next stage, negotiating with the enemy.

As we watch Antony fighting the pull of his enslaved heart, we cannot be quite sure of where the queen stands in relation to him. You think she's not aware of his sluggishness? Antony strides into III.vii amazed that Caesar's fleet has moved so rapidly. Her perceptive rejoinder?

Celerity is never more admired
Than by the negligent.

He takes the rebuke on the chin, like the man he is.

He has come back. She has *'nodded him to her'*, abandoning his new wife as readily as he did poor Fulvia, and just because she can, she exerts her power over him, offering him her support for a naval encounter against the best advice of his generals. *'For that he dares us to't'* is his inadequate retort to Enobarbus' furious query after vainly pleading for a land battle. And as for her personal involvement in that battle, her motives are resoundingly Elizabethan:

> *A charge we bear i' th' war*
> *And as the president of my kingdom, will*
> *Appear there for a man.*
> *Speak not against it*
> *I will not stay behind.* (III.vii)

Shades of Elizabeth at Tilbury? And indeed, harking back to military women, what turned Antony's world upside down in the first place but his late wife Fulvia getting up to no good in the field?

The queen's exit from the sea-battle is disappointing, but god knows it must have been utterly terrifying. I forgive her for it, and I sympathise; all that blood, those screams, those bucking ships and swamping waves. There is some historical evidence that both their ships were charged with sails ready for a clean get-away, since she was carrying her vast treasure with her in case of defeat. His exit, however, cravenly following her sails, is quite another story and a far greater humiliation for a seasoned general. Yet, in defeat Antony's shame is so heroic it almost becomes a moral triumph.

She shows her shame in a single tear (III.xii). He shows his love in kissing her for shedding it. Her repeated mantra, *'pardon, pardon'* is the one word adequate to express her guilt. No pretenses, no play-acting. When she looked back from the stern of her fleeing ship and saw Antony hoist sail and follow her, she must have been quite horrified, but such an act of cowardice, such a fatal pull toward her addictive presence, I bet would not have occurred to her vis-à-vis him. He is wrong, she didn't *know* he'd follow her; she is a very different animal from him and not drugged with passion as he is. She might have feared it, knowing him better than he her, but wasn't thinking clearly in the maelstrom of battle, her own terror being greater than her circumspection. That's only human.

Now, back again in III.xiii, as their world totters, she is ready to *'pack cards with Caesar'* to ensure her own survival and her heirs' succession. When Antony discovers her shamelessly, yet politicly, flirting with Caesar's messenger, she plumbs fathoms of hyperbole to wriggle out of the hole. This is an important device. For a Shakespearian actor, the most useful sense to develop is an unerring nose for truth and falsehood in a character's self-revelations. Do we always tell the truth about ourselves? Do we lie with a fervency equal to our desire to be believed? What instinct comes into play that tells a cornered character it's OK now to come clean – no more revenge, no more danger, a deep need to cleanse the moral palette?

At this juncture in the scene, after Antony has raged at her betrayal, it is not the moment for an admission of duplicity in Cleopatra's timeline; she still has a long way to go before being ready to *'rush into the secret house of death'*.

She is, however, guilty as hell. Her elaborate outburst of self-justification to Antony: 'rather-murder-my-son-and-ethnic-cleanse-the-whole-of-Egypt-if-I'm-cold-hearted-towards-you-darling', must, I feel, be taken with a large pinch of salt. This is how the most OTT speech in the play arises, just after Thidias, beaten half to death, is dragged out and sent packing back to Octavius:

> *Hence with thy stripes, be gone!*
> *Have you done yet?*
> > *Alack, our terrene moon*
> *Is now eclipsed and it portends alone*
> *The fall of Antony.*
> > *I must stay his time.*
> *To flatter Caesar, would you mingle eyes*
> *With one that ties his points?*
> > *Not know me yet?*
> *Cold-hearted toward me?*
> > *Ah, dear, if I be so…*

That quiet *'Not know me yet?'* covers the difference between them that I have outlined above. If he is mollified by her overwrought declaration of love it is because he so desperately wants to be, while to us she has revealed a royal expediency, shiftiness if you must, commensurate with her terror of defeat. Politicians will say the porkiest pies to save face, and a lover to convince a lover, and when both inhabit the same skin, there's a pretty potent mix of filler.

Defeat follows victory follows the final decisive defeat. Antony starts to fear her power over him with a mountainous aversion and becomes very violent towards her; she is scared stiff and runs away. This is the only scene in the entire play when the lovers are left alone onstage together, and it's murderously violent (IV.xii). It's as well to underline that this play is enacted in public, with witnesses looking on throughout, except for this very brief and incandescently potty scene. Antony alone has a long moment onstage before his death, and it is unique. The internal life is not presented to the audience as does Lear, Hamlet, Othello and Iago, the Richards, the Henrys, Macbeth, etc. You have to delve and glean in this play, and I can only repeat that the magic casement opens only very briefly. Keep the truth-telling radar at full strength. (Sorry, forgive the tumble of images...)

Fleeing in terror from the cornered lion, for once Cleopatra is visibly at a loss, and cunning, pragmatic, guard-dog Charmian throws her a cruel lifeline: *Send him word you are dead'*. She picks up on that lie, orders Mardian to tell it to Antony, and they hot-foot it to the protection of her monument. *Sauve qui peut.* He would never have done this wicked thing – she would: more proof of the unbalance between them? She thinks better of it, too late. That unthinking lie, received in all innocence by Antony, clears his mind of all thought except death so he can join her in the other world. It inspires in him the greatest quatrain of love-poetry ever penned:

> *Where souls do couch on flowers, we'll hand in hand*
> *And with our sprightly port make the ghosts gaze.*
> *Dido and her Aeneas shall want troops,*
> *And all the haunt be ours.*

This battered man achieves magnificence at last.

In her turn, when he dies in her arms, her poetry too begins an unmatched flight, as if such a man can only be realised once he's melted away. The verse becomes transcendent, elevated, as we watch her reaching for an understanding of herself, and her love, and her loss, and how ordinary that makes her: *'No more but e'en a woman…'*. She understands, too late, the magnitude of what is now gone from her. Just as Lear learns he is a poor forked animal, merely a man, before being a king, so does Cleopatra learn she is no more than *'the maid that milks'* before she is a queen.

Allow me to dwell on this signal moment in the play. There is a stage direction that appears without fail in all editions of the play that I have seen, at IV.xv, line 69. If it's not 'Swoons' it's 'She faints'. It's not a stage direction that appears in the First Folio, and which editor it was in the whole long line of them since then who inserted it I don't know, but the finger points to a mere man – sorry about this. I cannot think that any self-respecting female scholar would reach the conclusion that just because Charmian's and Iras' speeches appear to describe a silence, it follows that Cleopatra must have fainted dead away, like some girly heroine in a bodice-ripper. Cleopatra is not a swooner – rather more of a bolter judging by her behaviour at Actium. Plus, in girly romances when they wake from a faint they tend to murmur 'Where am I?' in wobbly tones. In this play when the queen stirs from her silence she speaks not at all like someone deprived of blood in the head, but like someone who has had a blindingly clear revelation of her place in the scheme of things. The philosophical idea is thoughtfully placed and fully expressed:

> *No more but e'en a woman, and commanded*
> *By such poor passion as the maid that milks*
> *And does the meanest chares.*

So I suggest that Cleopatra, not fainting away out of a situation but on the contrary, facing it squarely to consider her new reality, recedes behind a wall of silence, perfectly still, suddenly unattainable, hieratic as a figure carved in stone. The stillness and privacy of a figure lost in deep meditation overwhelms the stage. No wonder the women are disturbed by her silence. (It's as well to flag up that Cleopatra is not a westerner, but an Egyptian for whom both murder and meditation are daily bread. Her exotic persona is as important a reminder in the telling of this story as is Othello's exotic presence in that play.) Cleopatra returns from her meditation to comfort a weeping young Iras and to acknowledge her parity with her women. Her loss of power is painfully acknowledged; a thoughtful survey of what to do next follows; the idea of her own death is broached. That's a huge step for one so very alive.

Her journey continues into the last great act of the play where she doesn't give up on a viable future until she absolutely has to, turning and twisting in her encaging monument like a baited bear as the Roman dogs come sniffing. Her decision to kill herself is made incontrovertible only after a renegade officer of Caesar's, Dolabella, slips back to her monument to give her word that Caesar intends to bring her and her children to Rome for a triumph. That's the turning point in Cleopatra's journey. A triumph would be an untenable humiliation. Up to this point Cleopatra is open to political compromise to save her throne and the succession.

The Seleucus incident is usually cut in this final scene, but it is better for it to remain, a little trimmed maybe, so the audience gets the full gamut of her politic squirmings. All works by contrast; the scene will underline her bravery thereafter. It's the little interpolation where she presents her treasurer, Seleucus, to Octavius with a list of her treasure, and Seleucus, seeing which side his bread is buttered in the new dispensation, reveals the queen has kept back as much as she has admitted. She pretends shock and shame. Or does she? Did she plan it to convince Octavius of her wish to live? The critics who read these slithery incidents as shallow or 'womanish' need to rethink. The various historical interpretations of these final happenings, Caesar's motivation for one – did he or did he not want her dead? – have no place in the actual drama, but they make for fascinating extra reading. Our concern must be to get rid of the popular jargon about Cleopatra, and restore some depth to her heart, and animal intelligence to her brain. Yes, of course it still has to be a great love affair for heaven's sakes, but with nobs on.

Shakespeare offers yet another hurdle to the actress before he blesses her with nobility of spirit and inner resolve, the scene where the clown (it will have been the comedy guy who played it in Shakespeare's company), or the snake-man, or the fig-man, brings her a basket of killers, asps hidden in fig-leaves. There's no line to say he knows who he's talking to. (No doubt several palace servants died ghastly deaths on Cleopatra's orders before these snakes were decided upon as the best choice for a quick end.) Shakespeare pulls black comedy out of his hat with such daring it takes your breath away: a woman, simply dressed, nervously jokes with a strange fellow from the souks, giving nothing away. She herself is about to become *a dish for the gods*, and yet she sits and chats with the man about dying and pain. When he's gone she is ready to crown herself anew, to proceed with grace and majesty towards the final act.

Great tragedy must allow us to share the journey of the protagonists, and there is nothing paltry about these last enactments of the lovers' voyages, no lack of soaring poetry, inner substance, moral beauty. Nor those final touches of genius from Shakespeare where he sends his heroic creature swooping down for a few heartstopping seconds into the streets of common humanity, where a woman suckles:

> *Dost thou not see my baby at my breast*
> *That sucks the nurse asleep?*

murmurs the Queen of Egypt as snake poison floods her veins. Similar moments of bare simplicity are scattered throughout the late plays as Shakespeare becomes ever more attuned to magical flourishes of unexpected naturalism. He's a gob-smacking surrealist. Go figure.

As to her love for her dead Antony, it is only moments before her own death that she finally 'marries' her lover:

Husband, I come!

Now to that name my courage prove my title!

The love affair, impossibly vexed in life, is to be duly consummated in eternity. Only right here at the end of the play, and only then, we seem to see parity between the lovers. It's not that she doesn't love him throughout, but she loves her throne more. She is the arch-survivor who in the end can't make it, but by god, she tries.

So, about her in reality. She was the daughter of Ptolemy XII, descended from one of Alexander's generals, a Macedonian called Ptolemaus. She probably took the throne when she was about eleven years old, but had to be married to a male consort in order to govern; this was her brother Ptolemy XIII, who she soon got rid of. She died in unclear circumstances in 30 BC at the age of 38. Antony was sixteen years her senior, and he killed himself on August 1st 30 BC. Octavius, the grandson of Julius Caesar's sister, survived his opponents under his new name of Augustus for almost 45 years. The threat to his legitimacy of Caesarion – Caesar's son by the twenty-one-year-old Cleopatra, even though swiftly murdered by him – meant he made sure that all traces of Cleopatra were erased to ensure oblivion for her, and ensure a future reputation, the one he wished to promulgate, that of a whore. And so the sexually voracious image was launched. Pure spin. Latin and Greek historians, chauvinist to a man, were not averse, having as they did a rather 'eurocentric' view of the Middle East. So what's new? None of them spoke the languages anyway, which Cleopatra did, nor were they used to the idea of powerful political women. In a more equal world Ghandi, Meir, Thatcher, Merkel, Clinton, Lagarde, Aung San Suu Kyi help change the perception of women in office but it remains a minority phenomenon.

We don't know who her grandmothers or her mother was. We also know she spoke about seven languages – shades of Shakespeare's own Queen Elizabeth – including Greek, Latin, Persian, Aramaic and Egyptian, a rare monarch to have bothered to learn the language of the people. A smart move; she was adored.

She had learned to be politically astute first from her father, and then much later from Julius Caesar. She took him on a spectacular tour up the Nile on her famous barge, so he could see her as queen-deity in action. She would appear as Isis at the temples sited up the banks of the Nile, and had the devotional support of the priests. The Isis cult was very strong throughout the near east and into southern Italy. He seemed impressed with her well-ordered theocratic state. In July 46 BC Cleopatra visited him in Rome where she remained almost two years. She was given a huge villa outside the walls in Trastevere –

to appease Calpurnia probably – which gave him greater freedom to visit the queen. She had arrived in Rome with a large retinue among which were engineers, astronomers and academics from the Mouseion of Alexandria, outside of Athens the known world's main centre of learning. Antony and Cleopatra used Greek as their common language, Antony claiming Heracles as his ancestor, and preferring Athens to Rome – when he wasn't in Alexandria. She and Caesar spoke in Latin.

Her astronomer, Sozigenes, helped Caesar restructure the outdated, by two months, Roman calendar. Her engineers advised Caesar how to dry up the Pontine marshes which spread malaria. Inspired by the great Alexandrian model, a public library was planned – its first director, Varro, the writer. She must have caused a flutter in the dovecotes of Roman society with her fashions, her make-up, her style. This was the woman who could challenge old Cicero on literature and history, a woman in whom intellectual capacity, political acumen and culture were mingled to a quite extraordinary degree. No wonder the macho Romans resented her presence and her powers.

When Julius was assassinated by the conspirators (what dreams of empire was he toying with, inspired by her?) Cleopatra was pregnant and miscarried it is thought, before hurriedly escaping a tumultuous Rome and returning to Egypt. Later she would set her cap at Antony, a Caesar loyalist and Roman Etonian, so to speak. She absolutely needed a male consort by her side if she was to retain a throne constantly threatened from inside and abroad. And so, at the age of about twenty-seven, and bereft of Julius Caesar and the support of Rome, she laid her plans to ensnare and captivate Antony, aged about forty-two, on the River of Cydnus.

Unsuspecting, sweetly arrogant Antony was left sitting in the marketplace whistling to the wind while the crowds cheered her astonishing arrival on that fabled barge. For a few days after he had acceded to her dinner invitation, they seem to have entered a sort of mystic Nilotic union on those anchored ships; Shakespeare's uncanny instinct for the deepest recesses of human spirituality led him to this:

> *Eternity was in our lips and eyes,*
> *Bliss in our brows' bent; none our parts so poor*
> *But was a race of heaven.*

But that was then, before the play begins, and Cleopatra is evoking, in I.iii, that blissful state of passionate parity at the start of a great pairing, before dishonesty muddied it. What we meet as the play starts off is a woman disturbed by the fragility of their relationship, since Fulvia is still his lawful married wife. It is vital to emphasis the importance of marriage to the Tudor mind, and to the laws of the time; Shakespeare constantly invokes marriage as the ultimate haven for decency, honesty, openness, constancy, and a kind of equality for the sexes that the unmarried state cannot bestow.

So here's a cursory sketch of a woman determined to continue as her inheritance had dictated and quite unlike any we know today. In the Shakespeare canon, she is the only queen actually occupying a throne. Powerful queens we don't have any more, active plotters as queens we don't have, queens who might, at the flick of a finger, have been able to *'unpeople Egypt'* if she was so inclined, we don't have. Riches such as she had we don't have, the savagery of a savage age we don't have – well, we do, we see it all the time on television – but it's as distant to lucky us as the savagery of Elizabethan London. The physical understanding of such powerful entitlement needs attention paid.

She and Antony proceeded to have a pair of twins after Caesarion which delivers a prime element in the chemistry of the play: that she has heirs and hence an unignorable reason for trying every which way to assure the succession. (Think just how pertinent that was to Shakespeare's world with his wayward queen's perennial succession games.) In the play Antony calls his queen by her proper name: Egypt. He knew who she was. The person *is* the country in Shakespeare-speak.

I had an exchange of ideas about the balance of passion in the play with the historian Adrian Goldsworthy who in 2010 published his military history of this period, called *Antony and Cleopatra,* and this was his reply to my initial letter:

> Yes, I suspect you are right that in the end Cleopatra loves without reserve. She has tried the politics and tried to survive, even being willing to sacrifice Antony. That has failed and love, remorse, even guilt take over. She has been frightened all her life. Death at the hands of her family and their supporters was always a real possibility. She could also only have been lonely and isolated throughout her life. There was really no-one she could meet as an equal and trust. The closest she ever comes is with Caesar and then for a longer time with Antony. She needed them politically – and in many ways staying alive is about staying in power, and probably left little time for anything else – so it was never simple, but it is hard to believe that an emotional bond did not develop and grow stronger with time, even if at first she HAD to win over Antony as a pragmatic move. So the first instinct was to try to survive (and that meant some sort of political power at least for the children if not for herself) as she had been doing since she was a teenager. When that failed the closeness with Antony most likely assumed even more significance.

So here is proposed, by a grown-up, a grown-up story, made magnificent by Shakespeare, and significantly not reduced to a mere slavish sexual passion of Hollywood tinct. Having played it, I know how enjoyable it is to kick the old preconceptions up the wazoo.

Note: If, dear reader, you are interested in a blow by blow gloss on the text of the play, I humbly refer you to The Applause Shakespeare Library's *Antony and Cleopatra*, edited by Barry Gaines, acting commentary by Yours Truly, pub. 2001.

The Two Joans

I DON'T THINK *Saint Joan* is a *Hamlet*. I think Shaw's wrong. First of all, *Hamlet* is the greatest play ever written, and the greatest about death in all conceivable aspects. Hold it up to the light, it's a black diamond reflecting ideas about death and the concomitant unknown. Not as something gloomy in the least, but as something to be considered seriously by people who are alive. I don't think there's a scene in *Hamlet* that doesn't discuss the thing that happens in the end to every single one of us. The intellectual pre-eminence of *Hamlet* is unequalled in any drama.

Saint Joan is a sort of rogue play. As Judge Brack says: '*People don't* do *those things*'. Holy things don't usually happen to people. It's a very unfashionable voyage Joan is taking. Her spiritual largesse is untutored, instinctive, simplistic, faithful, cheeky; Hamlet's is tortured, sophisticated, poetic, philosophical, funny. They couldn't be more different.

But we know what Shaw means: he means this is a part that every actress must play. As an individual, Joan haunts us from the sidelines, but she's not central to our problems. When audiences watch *Saint Joan*, they're watching a sainted, blessed, tragic life, and powerfully tragic for being factual, but yet not one with which they can really and truly identify. And I suspect that as secularism informs our national debate more frequently, this play might appear increasingly out on a limb.

Parts for women, compared with those for men, are so few and far between that there are certain touchstone roles. Joan is a great part for a young actress. It's overtly spiritual unlike any other seminal role; her love affair with God is such an extraordinary one in being so intimate. Others at random – Masha, Sonia, Blanche, Phaedra, Hester, any of the girls in Shakespeare – are all too human, and their involvements are with themselves and the men in their lives. But Saint Joan has one thing in common with another real-life historical person, Cleopatra: both chose death over a compromised life. Hedda does too, but she's a fiction. Or at least as unfictional as Hamlet has become in the collective unconscious. The only unique aspect that I have to offer in these pages is that I have played in my time two very different Joans.

I was asked by Cedric Messina to do Joan for BBC Television in the Seventies. He was producing lots of major classic plays for the box, which doesn't happen much these days. In the Sixties, Shakespeare's Joan – called La Pucelle – was my first part with the Royal Shakespeare Company for its great quatercentenary *Wars of the Roses* season at

Stratford-upon-Avon, conceived by Peter Hall, when John Barton was directing the French sections of *Henry VI*. By the time I got to Shaw's Joan, I was ready to pooh-pooh the whole saintly business of it, because I had got taken by the Shakespeare one, so persuasive is he. He's incapable of writing something that you can't believe in, at least I find so. La Pucelle's protestations about being pregnant, her terrible lying, her cowardice, somehow rang very true to me, the response of a terrified child. I went into the witchcraft business in that period, quite extensively, and that, too, began to make sense – the way a young girl could become a prey to supernatural voices, could be lured by unseen powers, all that strange underworld, alien to us now, that Shakespeare plugs into with his witches and his ghosts. Mind you, Arthur Miller does the same thing, so it's not over yet with persuadable young girls, and malign 'grooming' on the internet fills us with terror for our gullible young. But the wiliness and spiritedness of the Shakespeare Joan rather took me. I rather liked her guile, even if she was nasty to her poor old dad.

Saint Joan is the better play about the historical Joan, obviously, but it's worth remembering that Shakespeare was a Protestant writing about a Catholic country and an old enemy to boot, so he went to town with a willingly Francophobic audience to play up to. Down to. Taking all that socio-political stuff into account, La Pucelle is still a really terrific little creation.

Some of the physical ideas I got playing La Pucelle drifted over into the Shaw a little, except that I had to abandon the witchcraft side for pure religious belief. I do remember struggling against the pull of sentimentality. One is always a child of the decade one is in, and the sixties were not famous for faith in God and religious fervour. Faith in drugs more like and vision-inducing substances. Subsequent decades unfold in Britain along the same lines, until by the time of writing it looks as if secularism, seen as atheism, has become threatening to some folk, and the Church of England is in a right bind. I don't find Dawkins 'militant' – I ask you, how can atheism do 'militant' having no burning arrows or godly swords to hand? – so much as a bit too sure of himself. My beloved mother always used to caution us with *'le ton fait la musique'* – 'the tone makes the music' – and someone needs to whisper it to him I suppose. I am perfectly at home with my adult atheism, although as an adolescent I wanted very much to be St Teresa of Ávila, fervently wanted to write poems like St John of the Cross, wanted to be pierced by arrows of desire. It was an arty thing really – well that's my story – but not a belief thing. Humanism won through eventually, as the hormones calmed down, though God does not enter any equations for me, Joan or no Joan.

This is the wonder of acting: you don't have to be what you act. But you do have to stop asking 'why' questions. We belong to a post-Freudian age; Shakespeare didn't. If you start asking all kinds of psychological questions, you're sunk. I found this to be true most specifically in the wooing scene in *Richard III* – Ian Holm was playing Richard. At first, I could not make sense of how that girl, Lady Anne, could be seduced by the monster who killed her father, killed her husband, and whom she loathed in every fibre of her being. At the end of the scene, how could she be at his knees, his for the asking?

Peter Hall called out from the stalls: *'Don't ask questions. Just do it!'*. He was right. You are not to ask *why* the wicked duke is wicked in *As You Like It*; he's just wicked, that's it. You're not to ask *why* Romeo and Juliet fall in love. They just *fall* – in love. So get on with it. The same thing with the emotional rush of Joan and her voices. She *heard* those voices. She *hears* those bells. She *believes*.

A weird thing happened. I was mulling one night over Shaw's stage direction: *'Joan makes her mark'*. I was in my bath – best place for thinking – and I was thinking 'What mark? What was the mark?' I thought no to an X, the normal cliché mark; too difficult if you can't write anyway to stop and change direction with the pen, too awkward when you are hot with shame. And I thought no to a thumb-print; she'd be ashamed not to take the offered pen. I thought: 'I know she didn't do that, I know she didn't. I *know* what she did, she made a circle!' An angry unstoppable circular scratch – one swift scrawl and it's done. And do you know, she did. I found that out later. The Paris archives have it all. No magic there, just common sense really.

The clothes too, I didn't want them shiny and classic like her statues in France, although I suspect Joan was rather vain about how she looked. I consumed books about her. They never help much when you're acting a part, but they provide the mental pictures. I have played many people who were once actually walking the earth: Joan of course, and Florence Nightingale, the Empress Alexandra of Russia, Edwina Mountbatten, Frieda Lawrence, Cleopatra, even Edith Swan-Neck for heaven's sakes, in my salad days when I had one. She was Ethelred's woman I think. You always feel you owe the dead something as they cannot speak for themselves. It's your duty to tell an objective and yet protective truth. Reveal but don't judge. The books flesh out the background which you're going to leave behind anyway, but in one instance, the private life of Alexandra of Russia; her maid, Anna Vyrubova, wrote some diaries which were helpful because she became a human being instead of a hated historical icon.

I think the hangover from *Henry VI* was this: La Pucelle was scruffier, a bit more lousy than the idealized one. She slept out in battles, and who was it that cut her hair? A bit of a little punk, my hair stuck up all over the place. As a child I had seen Ingrid Bergman in her film with that perfect blonde pageboy on that beautiful soft face. Her picture was on my wall at nine or ten, eyes gazing heavenwards, praying to her saints. I had a huge crush on her then, her burning was unbearable, I recall floods of tears. To be so holy and beautiful was devoutly to be wished. As an adult, I had seen Joan Plowright's Joan at the Old Vic and couldn't have asked for a better. Everything she did was perfect; that Lancashire voice bravely calling to her angels, those blazing brown button eyes challenging the world – unforgettable.

So I had to try another something when it was my turn. And because it was television and not the more rigorous stage, the realism was possible. Television likes naturalistic speaking, but there's no mistaking the long Shavian strophes, and that wasn't too easy to manage for me. I deliberately eschewed that Pre-Raphaelite looking-up-to-heaven thing of course. My Joan preferred to shut her eyes and conjure her saints like a child wishing for a toy, rather than to gaze upwards towards iridescent clouds. See them innerly where the camera could come close to search her face. I thought too, that unless the Dauphin had specially ordered a suit of chain mail to be made for her, whatever she had would be cast-offs, and would be slightly too big for her. Baggy. So things drooped a bit.

Still, whatever she looked like, it seems not to matter, because what was inside her was this glowing persuasiveness. You believe people when they are fervent about their beliefs, it makes yours seem so wishy-washy. Her soldiers did too. I liked also the flat sense of humour that pops up, and the practicality, in both Joans actually, but Shaw's more particularly. That common-sensical, no-nonsense tone of how things are. Probably it's Shaw's least intellectual and best play, because plain-spoken young Joan tamed his clever Irish arrogance.

John Barton and I were convinced that we should try to find a distinct accent for La Pucelle. They are totally English plays, the *Henry VIs*, nevertheless Peggy Ashcroft playing Margaret of Anjou chose to speak with a French accent. I can hear it now in my head, those ringing tones with that throaty 'r'. I might add here that Peg was iconic to me; there was a quality both naturalistic and spiritual about her acting because in her life she had a kind of blazing honesty and commitment to the causes she espoused. If she didn't believe something she wasn't able to do it. To me that was wonderful, to marry the two halves of your life so closely.

La Pucelle, though as French as Peggy's ringing Margaret, was a country bumpkin. Usually actors find a faux-Wessex or Mummerset drawl, or Welsh or Northumbrian – they all do very well, but they're very English sounding. We wanted something that sounded different, more foreign to the ear, a bit odd. Something that would make your ears prick up when she spoke. And so we plumped for Elizabethan. John Barton knows a lot about how they spoke, rhyme-endings and so on. It was great fun actually. Joan pronounced, like the Elizabethans did, *all* the vowels in diphthong words, as in earth – ay-ur-r-th – you hear every one of them.

John's party trick is to do *'Ill met by moonlight, proud Titania'*, and it would be 'Eel mate bay mo-onlicht, praud Titawnia'. The 'gh' now dropped, would have been heard, and also both the 'o's in 'moon'. It was those vowel collisions we were looking for. So La Pucelle sounded very weird, sort of English, yet not like any of the English side. A hard 'r', rolled rather than throaty, and those drawn out vowels. Fra-ance became a Big Name. Names are always wonderful – that moving list in *Henry V*. The way Shaw uses the word *'alone'* – I seem to remember drawing out that 'lone' syllable. They say now that Elizabethan sounded a bit like a Brummy accent, which would have been not unfamiliar to Shakespeare's ears, but we took it a bit further into oddness.

She came from a village where she would have had people around her all the time. But the peculiar events of her life, hearing voices, commands from heaven above, would have made her seem to them a touch odd. I felt she must have been both puzzled by her voices and utterly accepting of them. But the loneliness – well, it's horrible, and yet easy to understand. But what an awesome thing for somebody so young and unprotected to come to terms with. To be quite alone, like that speech in *Measure for Measure* where Claudio imagines what death is like, caged in ice, I needed to play it like that, but without the imagery that Shakespeare offers up. Play it as if the ideas were just coming out of her at that moment. Intolerable.

I don't think the tomboyness of it interested me because what happens when you wear pants or indeed chain-mail is that you naturally alter your body. With those fountains of lace cuffs in a Restoration play you naturally lift your hands in that wavy way so the cuffs don't slop into your soup. So when you wear rough clothes they tell you how to be. No cleavage, no flirting. She had lived a country life, was very basic and intuitive. As to the way she talks to the dauphin, the archbishop and the other church lordlings – if you are being spoken to by saints, then no king, no prince of the church, no lord, no officer is going to impress you very much.

The first scene is tricky. It's always fine once she becomes whatever it is she's got to be – persuader, soldier, crusader

– and thence one of the boys. But when she's neither fish, flesh nor fowl, when she's still in her kirtle and has not performed any miracles yet, that scene is difficult to gauge the temperature. Mawkish. Are you self-assured or shy, assertive or modest? Plain speaking seemed the way in. Simple. A messenger.

Telling Dunois about the voices was like a big secret. For the first time she more or less says, 'You will never understand it, I don't even understand it, but this is what happens'. I think I was so in love with that speech that I romanticised it a bit. To me she actually saw the saints in her mind's eye, and they were very classic, mediaeval manuscript figures, always bathed in oceans of light. These things do cross your mind about what is saintliness, and why do better people emanate perceptible auras of likeability, of humour, of wisdom, of earnestness? And indeed the origins of the halo in religious art, where does it come from? Apparently, in some instances, certain people have been blessed, maybe cursed, with being able to see the electricity we all give off. I knew an old actor who could see auras; it was a burden to him as he could tell when a person was ill, and also when an aura was a lousy one, too dark or the wrong colour so you weren't in the top class of persons, so to speak. When I learned all that from him one day I felt uncomfortable as if my goodness quotient was in need of a service. Holy people do that to one, as if they've got the answer. Joan did that to many people, which is non-historical, unprovable, takes no belief system into account, but would psychologically account for their cruelty to her. In science fiction movies we have the idea of stellar aliens giving off light and auras. Her saints seem to me similar.

We played the Loire scene on two horses and a camera up on a dolly to film Dunois and Joan on horseback. We were beside some English river, and we did see the wind change. That was lovely, I remember the pennant. That's always a great moment when the wind changes direction, so dramatic. Just think of *Iphigenia in Aulis* and the boats waiting to sail for Troy. Or the Armada smashed to bits on the bleak Irish coastline.

I remember that Keith Baxter, as Dunois, handed me the flag, Bourbon blue with the fleur-de-lis – a big moment and the tears were running down our faces, it was all working beautifully. Then we turned our horses towards the brow of the hill, cloaks flying, towards Orleans. But my horse went one way and his horse went another.

Mine was a vile horse called Kate, a grey, who hated me I could tell, ears back, an attempt or two to bite my foot with her big yellow teeth, and she headed straight for a pair of trees on the horizon growing very close together. I knew she was saying to herself 'I'm gonna get you off me', and she went straight for the middle. I grabbed her mane and stayed on, don't know how. And I heard this wild elfin laughter behind me: the camera crew on the dolly swinging the camera ninety degrees of the compass trying to film both of us. We had to trot back, contrite, and do it all again. But the tears didn't come so well this time, we were laughing too much.

I *loved* the trial scene, because it is, as we know, the real thing. That made me feel very peculiar, I must say, that voice emerging from the centuries. I found the trial the most emotionally effortless scene. It swings you along in a great wave.

No that's not quite true. Those sentences of Shaw's are too long, very Shavian. They go on and on and on. We broke for lunch, and John Gielgud, playing the Inquisitor, came to me and said in that wonderfully diffident articulated tone of his: *'Do you mind if I say something?'* 'Oh no, Sir John, no, please do', I grovelled. And he said – the best note ever – *'I think you'll find that Shaw has only one stress per line'*. And walked away to have his lunch. I stood there, stunned. 'My God, he's right'.

No lunch for me, back to my text, and in those long, long sentences there's the important word and you have to find it. I had been floundering. I wanted every word to be as important as the next. No. I had to let some go, and let that really quite simple mind hitch itself to one particular word or idea. Incredibly useful note. An actor's note to an actor. I thank him for that.

We used the Epilogue for the BBC film. I fought about it because I had thought 'Enough! The story is told. We don't need the happy coda'. Murray Melvin was the Dauphin. But anyway the BBC purists prevailed.

For the last line, I wanted to leave the audience with thoughts of Hiroshima. Atom bombs. Sanity. It's a good line: *'O God that madest this beautiful earth, when will it be ready to receive Thy saints? How long, O Lord, how long?'* It doesn't have the ordinariness of the last line of *Uncle Vanya* – that great surge which has such a heartbreaking optimism to it. Shaw is too rhetorical for that, but if one could get that surge into the last line it would be the feeling that we must go on doing good things, however long it takes.

How long is it going to take? Well, how long are people going to go on being unspeakable to each other? It sounds like an aria, but I think the meaning can be there strongly, made a tad easier on television because you can think it as an intimate soliloquy straight to the audience, looking them straight in the eye as it were. I can't remember now whether we did that or not, but the opportunity is there to ask them out there watching you, *the* question.

Her spirit speaks to us. Tremendously so. I think that's what I meant by saying the trial scene really used to get to me. Those mysterious phrases of hers: *'If I am in a state of grace, may God keep me there'*. I so believed that voice. What Joan had was something that most of us, I guess, in our less rational moments, envy. She had unthinkingness, absoluteness. Not weighing up both sides of the question as we must do, as she's got neither the time nor the inclination to see both sides. I recall Pier Paolo Pasolini's film *The Gospel According to Saint Matthew*, and the hurry that Jesus was always in, speaking to his disciples while he walked, his words carried behind him on the wind. It's a bad politician who thinks too carefully, though a wise man. The narrow focus of great leaders – Alexander, Napoleon, de Gaulle, all of them – gives them their fervency. She also had the fervency of her youth. My goodness if those youthful hormones turn to god instead of sex you have mountains of energy! Not sure that's a fair substitution…

She fights to the very end. I don't think she's a stoic, nor do I think she's fatalistic. She's terrified of being imprisoned, of being alone, and most of all of being burnt. Never could see the consequences of her calling, she simply had to obey them. When things blew up in her face, she was truly taken aback by what she had done and by what others did. That young terror, that shock, and her battle with that, is very touching. Do believers know that they are saintly? The whole thing is a mystery.

Hedda Gabler

THE FRUITLESS SEARCH for the Hamlet for actresses goes lurching along, and of course there isn't one, but this play will do very well. Better than Saint Joan as a candidate. I deeply regret leaving Chekhov out but in any case not to include Ibsen in a little book devoted to the other best playwrights ever would be remiss to say the least. In *Hamlet* death also appears strangely desirable. But where Shakespeare ponders and illumines, Ibsen implies. It is a subtext of utter genius. Also it brings us slap into the twentieth century, where subtexts are the order of the day.

I hope, dear reader (I have always longed to use this friendly address), you will forgive me if I flaunt just a little but I feel the need to justify a chapter as personal as the one I'm about to embark upon. I am acutely aware that this play has been dissected brilliantly before. Critics and scholars have written of it with perspicacity and indeed other actors may have recounted their stories, specifically Elizabeth Robins more than eighty years ago, but I had the great fortune to have caught the Hedda bus twice, and all I wish to report is part of the journey I took. An earlier Hedda that I did for BBC Television, before the later staged version, was a more jokey, malicious, superficial creature, teasing her way to perdition, by no means stupid and with a laconic humour conveying a sense of how clearly she sees her world. The second time round, I delved a bit deeper, and this time the world is anarchic, you are blown hither and yon by the prevailing winds that spring up, you have no power over events. Hedda hates that. A kind of fatalism about the way things have turned out gives her a strong sense of the absurd.

Sorry to swank: Prof. Peter Holland wrote to me in 1981 *'I think your piece on Hedda at the Ibsen conference is...one of the most brilliant accounts...of how an actor works towards a performance'*. If he of all people thinks this is useful it allows me to hope others, curious about the indescribable business of acting, might too.

I should preface this attempt at writing about acting by warning the unwary that it's a contradiction in terms. Gesture, tones of voice, expressions in the eye, the slightest physical reaction, can't be conveyed in words without being ponderous. And stage-time is ruthless; where I dwell here I flew on the stage, and conversely a brief exposition on the page can be a south-sea of discovery there. Hedda herself will not stand definition, yet that is true of any great play; its greatness is defined by its elusiveness. That is Hedda's secret strength; she deliberately evades definition by removing herself from the equation, the little devil, and so in the end she triumphs. Her friends are confounded, her enemy cheated and the free spirit roams in Hades. A Phyrric victory, arguably, but a blow for free will.

This talk was given at the University of British Columbia in 1978, and was published as *Ibsen and the Theatre: Essays in Celebration of the 150th Anniversary of Ibsen's Birth*, edited by Errol Durbach. My contribution is the sole actor's one amongst a brilliant roster of academics, including the great Michael Meyer whose translation we used in performance at the Duke of York's and for the BBC.

Would you be good enough to bear in mind the following few personal maxims? On the whole, to most people, the process of acting is unfamiliar, and this is *not* addressed to actors; they go their own sweet way.

a) You cannot act concepts, abstractions, or theories. You can't *act* an Oedipus complex though it might emerge as a concept to the sort of mind on the lookout for one.

b) What Ibsen might have intended I see only on the page of the text. If this play were by Anonymous, found in some attic, it would be the same.

c) From the actor's viewpoint, realistic drama is not 'realistic'. Hedda is no more 'ordinary' than Juliet or Millamant, not ordinary at all. I've never met a Hedda, though semblances abound in every suburb.

d) All drama deals with characters in a state of crisis. The longueurs of life are contracted into action. Even the seductive non-happenings of *The Cherry Orchard*, where protagonists refuse to resolve the crisis, are active.

e) Acting is acting is a rose is a rose, be it in bare staccato prose or lyrical poetry. It requires the same concentration of forces to convey meaning in one word as it does in a line of iambics. The classical actor is one who has made the joyful discovery that words are not scary things.

To examine a play of this calibre with any degree of thoroughness you need a month, preferably more, working six hours a day, maybe more. The chemistry of playmaking – the personality elements of all cast members interacting – is the essential catalyst that brings the thing to life. Clearly I can't deal in detail with the other six people who appear under the Tesman roof lest I unbearably lengthen my stay on these pages, so I have elected for the selfish point of view. It's what we all do in life anyway – see the world from our point of view – and partisanship is the vital protective stand one takes to give one's character the dignity of selfhood. Each character must be in the right for himself. It is up to the director to balance out those strong selfhoods to give his production balance and give it an overarching conceptual 'take'.

Enough said. I like Francis Bacon's (the painter not the other one) description of art as *planned accident*. I will try to share with you as much of the planning for this particular accident as I can.

The Paradox of Hedda: Not only must the actress present Hedda, whose inner scenario is awfully strong, but Hedda herself must present Hedda Gabler's outer scenario, which is equally strong. The one without the other is a cop-out. The former is for the audience so they can identify with her dilemma, the latter for the other characters so they may be confounded by it, and thus bring themselves as characters to fruition. A little like Hamlet sane playing Hamlet mad to confuse and gain time. But if there is any hint of her being *out of control* to the other characters, the last line of the play will be unworkable.

I had scribbled on the front of my playscript a fraction of a poem by Verlaine:

> *Et je m'en vais*
> *Au vent mauvais*
> > *Qui m'emporte*
> *Deçà, delà*
> *Pareil à la*
>
> > *Feuille morte*

[I waft / with the bad winds / carried here, carried there / like a dead leaf.]

It sounded like Hedda's epitaph and went straight home because if I had understood one thing about Hedda, it seemed that she had a heart. Maybe too much for her own good. I got no feeling of frailness from her, rather too much life. But she seemed prey to *accidia*, an old word now out of use, so perhaps post-feminist busyness has indeed changed women's lives immeasurably for the better. I recall a small Impressionist pastel of an elegant creature lying on her chaise longue in a curtained salon, head resting on elegant hand, staring at nothing; titled *L'heure Bleu*. The French use the mood less shamefully: *'l'accidie'*. We just call it depression, Churchill's 'Black Dog'. But that's a clinical description; Hedda's is a less definable restlessness, which makes her see the autumn leaves outside her window not just as melancholy, not autumnal, not exquisite like Vanya's autumn roses, but withered. No, she's not inert, she has energy to expend.

A prisoner of her heart then? Impulsive? Not an adjective often ascribed to Hedda who seems to be thought of as calculating, but I knew it was the one for me.

I have mentioned that an actor must become partisan about her character. You must defend that character, love her as you love yourself. But one thing was becoming clearer; if Hedda was merely a calculating animal, merely unreasonably malevolent she was an unworthy individual. So I began to wonder what demon winds were blowing her about? What pained her? What does she find worth defending, if anything? What bored her? What did she love? What excited her? When did she lie? When tell the truth? What made her laugh? (That's always a key discovery – if you don't find what makes Kate laugh you really shouldn't go near *The Shrew*, unless it's *The Shrew* as sociology.) What made her cry?

As I said, I've played this part twice, and previous to this exploration it was on the television: Waris Hussein directed it, Ian McKellen was Tesman, Jane Asher Mrs Elvsted, Tom Bell was Lovborg, Dorothy Reynolds Aunt Juliana, and Brendan Barry Judge Brack. But the annoying thing about television is that no sooner do you get a glimpse of other paths through the underbrush than the game is over. Done. Recorded. So I came away from it longing for another go. Luckily I got the chance, and this second stab had a healthy run at The Duke of York's in 1977. John Shrapnel – Tesman, Jonathan Kent – Lovborg, Rosemary McHale – Mrs Elvsted, Ian Bannen – Judge Brack, Gwen Nelson – Aunt Juliana, Renee Goddard – Berta. Directed by Keith Hack, set by Maria Bjornson.

So now. You think back over the high points in the play: the hat, the pot-shot at the Judge, making Lovborg drink, pulling Thea's hair, the burning of the manuscript, giving Eilert the gun, the final shot. But what about the bits inbetween? I'm consumed by curiosity: what made her do these things? Ask an audience what leads up to these haunting events and not one of them would be able to tell you with accuracy, just outrage. *'How could she force him to drink knowing he's an alcoholic? She gave him a gun to shoot himself! She burned his book! Callous! Unpardonable!'* On the defensive by now, I'm saying 'she's no Iago, there's *reasons and I shall find them!'* And so you loosen your hold on objectivity and allow that blessed selfishness to engulf you. You're on Hedda's side at last.

Each one of us, thinking back on a bad moment in our lives, shudders at the memory, but deep down we know why it happened. Like the car accident, there is always a version full of detail and self-justification. Hedda never falls asleep at the wheel. But what exactly is the story she might choose to tell? It is my job to find out.

A critic must start a thesis with a full knowledge of what has been written about his subject before. I propose that an actor should be innocent. Not ignorant but innocent. You read a lot around the work if you feel the need, but that's usually for historical characters. Photographs of the period are specially useful. They tell you of clothes, strictures, deportments, manners, taste, interiors. Julia Margaret Cameron's portraits will tell you as much about Victorian women and how they saw themselves as many a novel. There are very few plays that have passed into the arena of being public property, like *Hamlet*. This is another. What that means is that people feel they know the play intimately, somehow it belongs to them. Well, no, because you can't know a play, and I'm talking the Biblical sense here, unless you've played it. Like you can't know a lover unless you've slept with him. Nothing will help you reach that intimacy except the text itself. So to the text you go – and to the devil with preconceptions.

I don't speak the language but I skimmed through the play in Norwegian, and was struck by its verve and simplicity. Ask me how? I once went to the Maly Theatre in Moscow and sat through a Lear, and was struck by how well it sat in the actor's mouths; they seemed at home with it. I found out later the translation was by Nabokov so of course it was good. Anyway, *Hedda* in its own language: no long words, banal everyday phrases (I guess a knowledge of Afrikaans helped me get the gist), a proliferation of expletives like *'Good God!'* – no French in the conversations with Brack, just one or two words of Danish, I was told, to denote sophistication or 'in-talk'. It was the sophisticated neighbour to Norway, as France to us, so in English translations French is used as their common snobbery. So, after all, small-town Hedda and small-town Brack were a bit less fancy with their small-talk than the English versions make one think. Natural-sounding words, idiosyncratic.

Of course there are many difficulties in any translation, like the famous one of where exactly Eilert Lovborg shot himself. I consulted the good Dr. Jonathan Miller about this choice of word, although we know quite well where Ibsen meant; in what one might call the lower living quarters. *Unterlivet* it is in Norwegian – sitting below the liver – so we want a euphemism for that. (The liver is called the liver because it was thought that was where we lived, close enough to the stomach, where all emotions are felt, to have been readily confused.) 'Well, under the liver is the hypochondria. Shot himself in the hypochondria doesn't quite do the trick, does it?' Loin, bowel, stomach, balls, 'down there'. We used 'bowel'. Bannen's understated delivery of the word did the trick perfectly. Hedda nearly threw up.

'Read my plays carefully' says Ibsen, and this injunction is best obeyed lest you miss a trick. The play is constructed like a first-rate thriller, Ibsen scatters clues all along the way, and you must find them, and help the audience find them. It's not a play easy on the ears, poetry is lacking, and anyway most of us don't listen very hard, ready with a riposte before our interlocutor has closed his mouth. Nothing is cuttable, every word counts. Every word a character utters springs directly out of what another has just said, none of those seductively atmospheric Chekhovian non sequiturs. The only poetical exception

is the image of *'vine-leaves in his hair'* made by Hedda, a secret code understood only by Lovborg.

The vine-leaves: her own heated vision of him as a Greek god, when really he was merely a bohemian occasional visitor to her house. I like to imagine she must have come across a picture, maybe the ravishing Bacchic statue in the Bargello, in a book in her father's library, a memento of his own Grand Tour and far more interesting to her than his endless volumes of military history. No doubt modestly fig-leafed, yet that image would have embodied for her an irresistible notion of a free-thinking, free-drinking free spirit. Theories about the Dionysiac world-view, the zeitgeist, or whatever scholars like to play with, basically boil down to a young girl's over-heated adolescent take on the visitor. It's a view that fades between the end of Act II and the end of Act III. At that point, when there's a job to be done, reality takes over from the dream; the old secret ceases to thrill and is discarded. The figure of Death sneaks in to Hedda's little pantheon and takes up residence there.

These imaginative forays into Hedda's world before the play begins led me to invent a complete honeymoon itinerary – all six ghastly months of it. (I have it still in a pile of papers, but won't bore you with it; they had a dreadful fight in Bruges, and don't let's even think of the Dolomites.) That she'd plumped for the wrong man, that all her over-heated dreams about romance and passion were ashes, that George Tesman was who he was and couldn't be other, didn't even warrant a struggle any more. She took him because, as she says, he was the last one left. She was frightened of being left on the shelf, she'd married him out of cowardice. It's her cowardice that drives her; that honeymoon had taught her as much about herself as it had about her husband.

We decided to retain Jorgen and not the usual 'George', just to keep that slight oddness of a foreign household – a decision taken with Chekhov's plays where the patronymics are usually kept, lest fiery Masha become just plain old English Mary. The naming of names is particularly crucial: the derisory Auntie for Aunt, the rudeness in referring to Bertha as *the girl*, when is Lovborg called Eilert, the unsettling ploy of Hedda misnaming Thea, and Tesman persistently forgetting her married name, Thea being wooed into using Hedda instead of the formal address, the threat implied when Brack uses it, and the equal threat in his using her married name, the mockery when he elevates her from Miss Hedda, the daughter of his old friend, to Madame Hedda – thereby dwindling her into a wife. Most of all the moment when Eilert utters both her maiden names as if joining the two halves into an irresistible whole, not Hedda Tesman but Hedda Gabler, restoring her to full seductive power for a moment. Generals, professors, prime ministers, doctors –

in short all the petty bourgeois reverberations engendered by the very title of the play itself.

The play begins: what do you do, for heaven's sakes, when you get up in the morning very early, in a house new to you, a servant you don't know, a snoring husband still abed, father dead, no stables for a dawn canter, a life of tedium stretching to the crack of doom? Silence. Dawn light. I wondered about Hedda's so-called popularity. I don't think she has many friends; she'd be a girl who gives the impression of being so sought after that in the end no one asks her out. Her demeanour was perhaps off-putting. The line *'I suppose all our best friends are still in the country'* is one of the most forlorn imaginable.

Despised domesticity. And despised motherhood. The horror of being taken over by her pregnancy is perhaps the most important skeleton in Hedda's cupboard. Ibsen never dwells on it but he makes it very clear. However, George Bernard Shaw in his résumé in *The Quintessence of Ibsenism* fails utterly to notice this most central condition. Quite apart from Auntie's wink-wink hints, there are at least a dozen references made to it by Hedda during the play, starting with *'God, yes, September already!'* in Act I. Anyone who reads this as a botanical reference to the state of the leaves is barking up the wrong tree. It means quite simply that there are four months to go. No question of an abortion in those days. She's lumbered with a thing that will limit her from now till the end of her days. In that sense she is Everywoman, is she not?

And I can never forget, though Tesman does, that she kills two people at the end of the play. I found, in fact, that her pregnancy drew together every strand of the story so fundamentally that to doubt it for an instant would jeopardize the playing of it.

i) *Power* over other people: she has none over her child. It will grow and grow. She cannot influence it, cannot stop it, hardly knows how it began.

ii) *Sexuality*: her disappointment and bewilderment over what she imagined the act of love to be, and what it actually was are appalling. *'You haven't any idea about anything much'* she snarls at Tesman. Poor fellow – what could he possibly know.

iii) *Vanity:* like a monster, it will make her grow ugly and fat.

iv) *Physicality*: her loathing of being touched by people she finds unappetizing. Were she to admit it to Auntie, the cloying affection, the fond hugs from Tesman, knowing looks from Bertha, mockery from the Judge, would all be untenable. Being owned, being linked, no!

v) *Freedom*: the baby curtails even dreaming of that possibility more powerfully than a prison could.

vi) *Life* itself: it is a force that mocks her fascination with death at every turn.

vii) *Beauty*: her half-formed ideas of the aesthetic and the romantic are in danger of being made absurd by the baby's existence. You lie back, shut your eyes, and wallow in alluring and fearful dreams of Eilert. And it's not even his! It's terrible to be carrying the child of the man you despise while the image of the man you love is carried in your head. For love, read 'obsession' if you prefer, it's all one. *'Nothing serious has happened you mean?'* – the judge should only know! *'But for God's sake it was only a book!'* No one can say her priorities are seriously impaired.

viii) *Self-definition*: this unwanted thing has dared invade her life. *'I never jump'* she retorts to the Judge, but she has and it's horribly humiliating.

Not even Eilert must dare to explain herself to her: *'Careful, don't presume too far,'* she warns, don't get too close. The Yeats poem comes to mind: treading on her dreams. I believe she cannot equate living with compromise, and that makes her less adult yet more true to herself than anyone else in the play. I can't bear being regimented myself, and I instinctively understood Hedda's fear of predictability. Tesman will adapt, and find a way of resuscitating that book. Berta's dependence will mean she must adapt to whatever is meted out to her. Auntie will adapt to the death of her sister. Thea will do anything to adapt. Eilert tried and failed. Hedda cannot try and must not fail.

Paralysed by her own perfectionism, tied down by the lack of alternatives, devoured by the greedy lives around her and inside her, where is she to direct that animal energy of hers? She needs to be central to everyone's attention, she must know everything and commit herself to nothing. And what a commitment to the future that baby is! Her final act is an absolute necessity, and in that sense it is her sole act of passionate commitment. If that sounds too fancy, then she's just a cornered animal, and that's the truth of it.

Acting is a process of diminishing your choices, so that a course of action becomes inevitable. If a sort of encephalographic sensor were attached to the brain lobes during a performance, at any given moment the possible choices would be multiple. The same pertains in life as in art, you dodge that car without thinking in order not to be hurt by it. The actor is made aware, by rehearsing them, of the choices open to her, but the final decision must be driven by the unfurling nature of the character herself, and must appear incontrovertible. Edith Evans once said something like this: that if a bolt of lightning were to strike her at any point during a performance the resulting statue would look right for all eternity. The moment in other words, should be truthful. Well, we do what we can, we lesser mortals.

'Sometimes something comes over me. Just like that. I can't explain it' she confesses, and we watch her throughout the play saying and doing things which she cannot see the consequences of. Lady Macbeth has the same affliction. Hedda takes terrific chances, and then faces the consequences with a disarming candour. These strange, disturbing things she does, she does because she is ready for them. She is spoiling for trouble when she gets up that morning, and the first trouble she makes is with Auntie's hat. It accelerates from that moment on, and the final trouble she makes is shooting herself the following night. The action of the play is 48 hours. Very taught, tight, and classical.

Know anyone who would deliberately insult the taste of a kindly visiting aunt-in-law by pretending to mistake her hat for the maid's? She is driven to make mischief by the welcome lavished on Tesman's horrid childhood slippers. Hedda's version of morning sickness – which I swear she never has – is to be engulfed by cosiness. She didn't plan the hat business: the fury was there, the hat was there, the aunt was there…bingo! Then she has the gall to enquire of Tesman, not once but twice, if auntie might have been offended, and the gall to admit to Brack that she had done it on purpose.

Know anyone who would threaten to shoot at a visitor with a real live bullet in a primed gun, and then actually shoot? General Gabler's daughter was sure of her aim, one of her few accomplishments, but did she apologise for the fright? Nope.

Know anyone who would entertain the monstrous idea of burning someone's enviable head of hair, and then actually light a taper and move to do it? Simply for the hell of it. How gratifying to watch Thea's terror, and how lucky that Bertha interrupts. Well, anyway that's what I did; it seemed so at one with her nature. She dares all the time. It's a word occurring throughout the play like a leitmotif.

Know anyone who would help a person to kill himself? No, actually put the idea into his head, and the means into his hand? To her it's perfectly logical; if he wants to he must be helped. It will be his decision. She never apologises for that either.

Know anyone who would take a manuscript, to the writer his life-changing work, and throw it into a fire? Then later admit to the crime as wide-eyed as a bad child? (She might have done him a great favour; I have little faith that Lovborg's manuscript was the Norwegian *War and Peace*.)

Know anyone who would react to the death of a lover with undisguised elation? And then explain why, without a vestige of shame. Or who would admit to being an accessory to that suicide, and judge the man who offers to cover up her part in it as being dishonourable? Her so-called social conventionality is of a very unsentimental order it seems. She's a rebel.

Is this person a liar? If she is not, then what on earth is she doing? She is testing the waters of her life: testing, testing…is this life, what is love, am I powerful, how much will people take, how much can I take of myself, do I merit the gift of life, and if life is not a gift should I bother with it? The others in the house are the antidote to her own vibrancy, except for one, Eilert. The others hem her in, disgust her, bore her, annoy her, desolate her. They are the prose to Eilert's poetry – until he too turns prosaic. And to poetry – compressions, metaphors, mysteries, she responds.

Before we get to Eilert, bear with me a little longer about Hedda's desperation, her loneliness, otherwise the triad of her 'crimes' might seem too arbitrary, too heartless for us to bother with her. I'm talking of the drink, the gun and the burning. Let's see where she openly reveals herself. She does it covertly all the time, almost as if hoping for someone to find her out, but let's look at the overt declarations.

Act I: she is left alone and wordless – what you might call a silent soliloquy. Ibsen has his stage-direction but it's just his indication to show a restless, unhappy creature. I saw Tesman's slippers as I roamed around the cage of the room, and kicked them aside, hateful things. I saw the portrait of my father, and flew to it as if to draw comfort from the man who had left me unprotected, and then felt foolish at his lifeless stare. I felt claustrophobia closing in on me and went to draw the curtains aside and open the French windows, breathing in fresh air.

Tesman comes back in. Another young wife might have had the guts to say, were she liberated enough, at this point: 'Look, I hate this house, I hate your aunties, we've had six hellish months together and I think I see this marriage is never going to work' but she's not a Nora. Well, few people just walk out; it takes courage. She's pregnant, has no money of her own, no family house to run to. They live in a small town feeding off gossip, her father's respectable name would be smirched – the old boy from his stiff portrait is glaring at her now – she's far too proud to walk the streets and anyway too timid to envisage such a fate. She *needs* the safety of this place to enclose her fragile self-respect.

Society doesn't like mavericks, and we shall have to see whether society wins. Is this a dated premise then? I think not, since a norm is not being followed here. Drama likes mavericks even if society spurns them. Tesman tries to pull her into that society by offering: *'You're one of the family now'*. And her reply? *'I don't know about that'*. She is fighting the comfortable communality of marriage from the start, though hoping for the comforts it will afford. She has made her bed, and is having a devilish time lying in it. When she discovers her reduced circumstances at the end of Act I, well, anyone would be angry wouldn't they? The bargain is being traduced.

There is another 'soliloquy' at the beginning of Act II. Ibsen describes her readiness to receive visitors, and that she is busy loading her gun. So – we'll see the furniture has been moved about to her own dispositions, not Brack's. Father's portrait is now hung in that inner sanctum, along with her piano. That piano is about the only thing left from her own childhood, and it will speak right at the end of the play. The bowers of flowers from Brack are less profuse and placed as she wishes. She doesn't dislike flowers in general so much as Brack's bloody flowers, presaging – what? Now if they had come from Eilert…

The house is quiet. Tesman has gone out. Berta has her old feet up. Hedda has changed into an afternoon dress. I am describing the strictures of a Hedda in her own time, which clarifies her dilemmas, but another production in another period will find its own justifications. So, a dull day proceeds on its way. What will happen?

Is she expecting Brack? Is that why she's cleaning her gun? He knows her gun-training of old. Or is it just something to do that she's familiar with and gives her a small sense of independence? Being the only daughter of a military chap must have meant that horse-riding and shooting were part of her upbringing, and the freedom they gave sorely missed here. Too unsettled to sit down, I ran the butt of the gun down the piano keys. An ugly sound. I wandered round the sitting room, shoved the back of the rocking chair as I passed it. It rocked noisily on its own.

The clock ticked. I stood, unsure of what to do. Toying with time? Time toying with me? I began cleaning the pistol, checked the sights and turned to take mock aim at what – Daddy? His frozen glare caught mine. I took aim. Patricide! Don't bother you fool, he's well and truly dead. What might it feel like to kill yourself? I brought the gun to my own temple, interested by the cold feel of metal on skin, strangely desirable. I wondered if it looks as ferocious as it feels? I posed in front of the mirror as an actress might, I fancied. A stray wisp of hair annoyed me, spoiled the picture. Diverted from morbidity by vanity, I smoothed it back in place. I wished fleetingly I had hair like Thea's.

I heard the crackle of leaves from outside, and saw the Judge walking through my garden. The back way! How dare he? Too presumptuous by half. I shall give him a fright. So I did. This one minute charade exposed her dilemma most explicitly to me; emptiness, boredom, vanity, death, time. *'Well, what am I to do?'* she cries to the Judge. What indeed?

Lest all this description should appear as self-conscious as it reads, I should explain that doing this paper has forced me to look back at a performance and try to analyse in retrospect what I remember doing on stage. Force myself to remember. Try to recollect in tranquillity. It's harder than I thought it would be. Often I would do different things – hit a cushion instead of push the rocking chair – put the gun in my mouth instead of the temple – and so on, but the intentions would have the same aim.

The ensuing scenes with Brack are astonishingly frank. She answers everything with truthfulness. He pretends to be shocked now and then, but you don't believe he is. Intrigued, yes. She is what the French call *une allumeuse,* a lighter of fires; an arsonist might be the better translation. He is secretly delighted that a way seems to be opening up for him.

Why is she so disloyal to Tesman? The mischief of it titillates her, but I think she's tired of pretending connubial bliss, and having correctly gauged the extent of Brack's hypocrisy, is testing if she can trust him with her own? When she refers to *'our sort of person'* does she mean their common gentility or corruption? Is she also searching for some assurance from him that she might not have made as big a mistake in marrying Tesman as she fears? Should she hope?

A dark cloud settles on Hedda, a moment here, a moment there, incomprehensible to Brack's self-serving perceptions. *'My time was up. Oh no, I musn't say that or even think it'*, or again, *'This place smells of death'*. She's not that good at concealment: *'I have made my bed, I shall have to…I was about to say'* – a realist struggling to emerge; *'No obligations for me'* – losing the unequal struggle; *'Boring myself to death'* – the realist again.

I had thought, during the first few weeks of the play's run, that her sotto voce comment to Tesman's envious, yet generous, reaction to Eilert's new book:

'I could never write anything like this' was simply cutting. But I discovered that her *'Hm…no. No'* spoke worlds of sorrow and disappointment as she watches the two writers in her life.

Her self-dislike is overwhelming. *'Courage. Yes. Well that is the thing to have. Then one can survive anything'*. She is talking about herself, angry inside for what she knows she lacks. At the very same moment she's turning, swift as a lioness, on Eilert as if to say let's see if *you* have this vaunted thing. There is a tantalizing history between these two, and talking as they are in euphemisms, her cryptic line to him when they are reacquainting over the photograph album: *'That was not my worst act of cowardice that evening'* must mean she regrets ducking out of something that evening. My view of the incident: always electricity between the two of them, one evening he comes on to her, she's terrified and grabs one of Dad's guns, he runs away, she never forgave him for fleeing. Over the photographs, he at last understands what it is she wanted and what he failed to deliver that night long ago. It's a physical thing. But she resists being defined, even by him, and if there is regret in her heart she is too proud to show it.

When Thea comes in and the two of them seem to have secrets she is jealous of course. Her wild animal has been house-trained. She has to rock the boat. He cannot be owned by Thea, she has to be *'in the middle'*. Direct the show. Hedda proceeds to tease Eilert into taking what she knows he wants, and he takes it, he drinks. She's baited him, he baits her; these are old combatants and the spark is being re-lit. She despises him for that – it was all too easy. But the dream is always more attractive than the reality, and she must get him away out of sight, to her 'vine-leaves-in-his-hair' scenario.

'If only you could understand how poor I am and you have the chance to be so rich, so rich' she says to Thea, admitting to her own *'halfness'*, though Thea has no idea what's in her head. Here she despises her own nature most vulnerably,

and again in Act IV with *'Why does everything I touch become ludicrous and ugly?'*

But this show of desperation, eliciting unwanted pity from Thea, must be transmuted into a more familiar wickedness, games-playing. Hedda's games tend to turn disturbingly serious very quickly. She knows she can charm people, but she has a hunger to know if she can affect their lives or can she change the course of her own? Shall she not have a go at frightening Thea as much as she frightens herself?

I'm looking for the chinks in Hedda's armour where the light is let in for an instant, so we can trace the impulsions in her nature that drive her to do as she does. The bad winds.

Act III. Tesman says: *'I'm going to confess something to you, Hedda. When he'd finished reading, an ugly feeling came over me'*. Ugly? But that's my prerogative, she's thinking. You have ugly feelings too? The play is full of little repeated phrases like that, and they are for real shock and surprise, not for plot emphasis.

The line: *'But surely this could be re-written?'* when she asks Tesman about the MS she'll later destroy, went through many variations. Was it rhetorical since surely she must have suspected it couldn't be? Was she playing the innocent child to conform with Tesman's patronising paternalism, as if 'This is man's work, m'dear, don't bother your pretty little head with it' sort of thing.

Was it said to enrage him, by belittling the work of scholars? Or does she really and truly not understand and is being genuine? Hedda seems not much interested in books, her inner life is directed towards herself, and how modern an affliction is that?

Acting being the living thing it is, the manner in which I asked the question often depended on how much Tesman was hung-over after his partying, and therefore how much he was irritating Hedda. The important thing is that Tesman's *reply* makes the manuscript more precious and powerful an object for her consideration than it had been before.

Tesman asks her to come with him to see his dying aunt. *'No. No. Don't ask me to do that. I don't want to know about illness or death. I can't stand ugly things'*. Almost tearful with horror. I don't think it's a line lightly said, a fobbing-off of Tesman, she *means* it. Death seems so attractive, and her own fascination with it is Gothic-Romantic and nowhere near the unsightly wrinkled dwindling of honest folk. She can't envisage a gentle passing in your own bed, your loved ones around you; it implies a long and rewarding life for one thing, and hers so far is short and troublesome. She's twenty-eight by the way. To expend all this pain and effort on surviving from day to petty day and then to be denied a grand exit. No.

At the end of this scene, the crucial impulsion comes: the manuscript, now precious as the Holy Grail to her in its potential power, is in Tesman's hands.

He's about to have a nap and then return it to its owner. Almost negligently, she remembers the letter summoning Tesman to his dying aunt, so Tesman puts the manuscript down to read it. She can't take her eyes off it, it seems to be radiating malign power like a piece of plutonium. He becomes distracted with concern for his dying old aunt and begs her to come with him. She refuses swiftly and urges him to '*run*'. Another sort of tease; Tesman running is a cruel picture. The Judge is announced. The domestic flap-doodle at its height. Berta in a tizzy. Hedda longs for the Judge's gossip, and forgetful of poor Tesman, consents to see him. Tesman overlooks the manuscript on the way out. She reminds him of it, and he wheels back for it. She, suddenly covetous, hugs it to her and says she'll hang on to it for him. That seems acceptable so off he bumbles, bumping into the Judge on the way, and this diversion allows her to whip it under the sofa cushions.

God knows why. Some instinct says hide it from the Judge. He stretches out on that sofa, and Hedda has her secret, though what's to be done with it she has no idea.

But hey! – it's an intrigue and that's made the day less fusty.

She's deeper in blood now. A dangerous game, meddling with a man's life. *'Little fool, meddling with a man's life'* she's said to Thea. Thea, she thinks, all sweetness and solicitude, is blurring the hard edges of Lovborg, forcing him to be what he's not, domesticated. Like being loved by a marshmallow. That free will Hedda sets such store by because she has none, is being eroded by a mouse! Eilert is Hedda's peer and she does not like him being tampered with. She can see how dangerous it might be to toy with a man's better nature, and is scared of the outcome.

At the beginning of Act IV Ibsen again sets the visual scene with his Hedda dressed in black, walking up and down the darkened room. If a stage-direction is a good one it will tell you the author's vision, if it's a bad one it's a dictation and can be a drag. So, I obeyed Ibsen but added a cigarette. Peggy Ashcroft told me she had done the same as it was such a liberating thing for a provincial woman to do, so sophisticated and daring. So I wasn't breaking any new ground here. But maybe my intention was more to remind the audience of her pregnancy since the cigarette made her retch. She hadn't refused Tesman's offer of a cigarette in Act II for nothing. Here's a nice point: I'm aware that it's a very modern thing to know that smoking is bad for pregnant women, and that Hedda's generation would have known nothing of that, but old plays need still to speak to modern audiences, so sometimes they need a little contemporary jog. She goes to breathe fresh air again as she had that morning.

Auntie comes in and oh god, social niceties again, Auntie's description of Rina's dying sends her mind reeling back to her own satanic script. *'Oh, thoughts, you can't control them'* she has said. There's another revealing line in this exchange: *'You'll be lonely now, Miss Tesman'*. To be young and lonely is bad enough, to be old and lonely, no! They just might have found common ground here, but Auntie smothers the moment with hints about babies yet again and the fragile chance is lost.

'It's killing me all this, it's killing me'. In our production we went for it, where Hedda confesses she is pregnant. In the three scenes where Hedda and Tesman are by themselves, the public mask with no strangers present drops. To be brief, Tesman became so enraged to hear what Hedda had done with the manuscript that he began to strike her very violently. She was so shocked and scared at his anger that her initial desperate lie was as self-protective as it was mendacious: *'I did it for you!'* He, all flattered affection, says *'I never realized that you loved me so much'*, so she wades further into the mire, sickened by his gullible nature as much as by her own deceit, and attempts to tell him about the baby. His ensuing joy is too much to bear;

this is a woman being killed by kindness. Surprisingly, she laughs. It's all so ludicrous, she laughs. I'll come back to that in a moment.

I should address the two memorable events in the play – handing Eilert the means for his death, and killing his 'child' – burning the manuscript. They seem two souls at home with each other. No Thea present to muddy the waters. It is tragic to see two people missing each other who were meant to be together. The vine-leaves image has spent itself; they both are in doubt about the value of their own lives. He suggests his own suicide. She quite suddenly remembers how she can help to accomplish this; accomplish her dark dream of death: the pistols. He is not shocked by her gift of it. He accepts it with a simple *'Thank you'*. No melodrama, no sentimentality. She is restored in his eyes to the old Hedda, mistress of guns and horses. She calls him by his full name: a roll call of the dead. He responds with her full name, as he first knew her, Hedda Gabler. Her sole injunction is that he must do it beautifully. He responds gravely enough for her to believe that he will do it with the grace she craves. (So it's easy to read her desperate disillusion when she hears he's botched his death. It was to be either the heart or the head, but not 'down there!')

So now, left alone, trembling with the hope that he will end his life meaningfully she has one last great thing to do for him. She must complete the parable of the lost child. The only way to cleanse her life of him, his life of Thea, and both those of posthumous judgement, is to burn the book. All his drivel about it being a child is a risible indulgence to a woman heavy with the real thing. She may also have some unspoken awareness of both of them – the book and the child – being products of ill-matched unions. And the value of the work? Unpublished it remains a conundrum, published it would be assessable. I frankly don't believe Eilert when he boasts about it: *'My voice in every line'* (Act II). Compare Trigorin in *The Seagull* – there speaks a true writer it seems to me.

He certainly uses its loss to debarass himself of Thea: *'I don't want to live her kind of life any longer'.* After his line *'There's no future for her and me'* I felt gleeful no less. (I see I've slipped into the first person; that happens with actors.) My vacillation about whether to tell him the book was safe, was over. He left, I listened for sounds in the house, and then I moved irrevocably towards the burning stove, manuscript in hand. The hot door burned my fingers, the light and heat glared out at me. I waited for a surge of the old daring, took it at the flood and chucked the whole thing in. No delectating it page by torn page as I had done for the TV version. This Hedda was less light-headed, more driven by those demon winds. The flame caught, the edges curled, it hurt my eyeballs, I slammed the door shut.

I'm talking rubbish; it wasn't a real fire. But there you go, that's how it felt. I felt lighter, total destruction had liberated me to go down my own pathway – to push open the door to *'the secret house of death'* as it were. Now it was up to him. He was free. Unable to abort her own, she aborts Thea's 'child'. The burning always stays on in people's minds because it's so terrible but in Hedda's it is very quickly replaced by a far clearer flame.

Act IV is most miraculously written and constructed, not a word out of place. Hedda travels at first a murky and thorny trail, but when at last she bursts out into the open and spies the lie of the land, she sees her own salvation burning darkly. She hugs to herself the greatest power she has ever experienced, that of escape and liberty, conquers her *'halfness'*, cocks a mighty snook at all the provincial paraphernalia of which she herself had been fancied the very mark and glass, and takes her innocent babe with her into the dark.

She cannot be Auntie's sweet mother-to-be, cannot be Thea's confidante, cannot be Jurgen's faithful spouse, cannot be Brack's mistress, but by god she will be herself! Eilert's death done with the dignity she craved of him would have been a beacon, but he has only shown her how not to do it. A dread lightness comes upon her. Jokes come easily as she arranges her scenario with a sure touch. This time, bang through the head and no botching.

I was given by Peggy Ashcroft a most treasured thing, Mrs Patrick Campbell's creased, well-thumbed softback script of the play. She was given it by John Gielgud, who was given it by Mrs Pat herself. I donated it some years ago to The Theatre Museum so others could see it, but perhaps I should have waited a bit and handed that baton on to Eve Best, the best Hedda of late in my view, fully at home with Hedda's sardonic turn of mind, and light of touch. I have hardly any clues to the magic that Mrs Pat drew out of these pages, only a singular scrawl in pencil: 'Laughs', but not detectably linked to a line. And not where I thought it might be, at 'You Jorgen, your life!' But that general injunction to laugh is right. Hedda laughs a lot, self-mocking, mocking others, sometimes genuinely amused, sometimes bleakly at her own awful predicament. A sense of the absurd is a condition of her day.

So to the last lap of Hedda's journey. She has not found any respect for her husband. Judge Brack disgusts her with his innuendos and his bribes; insinuating himself once too often, the 'back way,' into her life, and at the end presenting her with an intolerable blackmail. Eilert, disfigured and shamed, roams, bereft of her vine-leaves in Pluto's shade. Thea and Tesman are made for each other, the resurrection of Lovborg their common goal. It's ludicrous! The way is open for her to free herself.

Ibsen has a stunning stage-direction that no one should mess with. *'People resign themselves to that sooner or later'* coos the Judge and *'She returns his gaze'*. After a moment she says: *'Perhaps they do. Perhaps they do – but I'm not "people".'*

Now, light and amused – a clear pathway always lifts the burden of indecision, rather like the Ranevskayas in *The Cherry Orchard* who feel lighter once the beloved house is sold – she touches things for the last time. The two heads bent over their hopeless task of rewriting a book by a man they don't understand. It's more than just amusing, it's funny. She plays with Tesman's pipe. *'Can't I help you two at all?'* she moues disingenuously, purposely disturbing their work like a buzzy fly to be swatted away. But this Tesman, perhaps dimly feeling a future ahead with a woman equally devoted to a posthumous shared endeavour, replied only distractedly. Their blonde heads bent over the shredded manuscript, they continued their labours. I have seen another Tesman, brilliant Benedict Cumberbatch to Eve Best's Hedda, as enraged as a lightning rod, leaping up to blaze with his suddenly opened eyes, seeing the real woman he had married for the first time. I still remember the violence, the force of his *'No!'* straight to her face.

This from Saul Bellow's *Herzog*: *'With one long breath, caught and held in his chest, he fought his sadness over his solitary life. Don't cry, you idiot! Live or die, but don't poison everything…'*

She never willingly shows that grief but it underscores the wild piano playing and the assured aiming of Dad's pistol to her temple, and the shocking end to a tiny provincial martyrdom. *'Good God, people don't do such things!'* Well, this one bloody well did. Ibsen's play is meant to be a shocker.

Gertrude and Ophelia

Two of the loneliest women in the whole canon of drama and yet the most crucial to the plot. Gertrude is clearly a woman enamoured of her new man. Ophelia seems OK with her brother's departure because an amorous adventure is opening up – Hamlet is back home and hot young bloods are stirring. But follow the fortunes of the two women and they will be cast into a kind of limbo soon enough.

Why should I be trying to mark the journeys of these two characters in the greatest play ever written? What do they matter in the turbulent course of Hamlet's tragedy?

Simply this: the two most sustained and passionate scenes in the entire play are with his lover and then with his mother. And in general, due to the intermittent nature of their appearances, these two pivots of his heart seem generally sketched in merely. Or that's the impression.

And god knows proper actresses have given their all in the playing of them. I recently saw a remarkably witty tour de force from Michael Sheen with absolutely zilch connection to these two women. Very dispiriting. No humanity. Shakespeare's plays respond so fully to human connections, and are diminished if you ignore them. Though depressingly most people don't notice as they're easily blinded by a star performance. Of course the temptation in playing Hamlet is to show off, in fact it's a sort of one-man show if you're not careful, and the women inevitably recede unless the director keeps a sharp eye. So *much* in the play to keep an eye on. It's so rich and so swift. The water gushes and sparkles. And although it explores death and dying at every turn it's never depressing. What a miracle! One of the best productions ever was directed by Buzz Goodbody, and then she killed herself just before the first night. Makes one think a bit.

First question for Gertrude: why did she marry Claudius so quickly? Second: why didn't she try to save Ophelia? Answer: 1: Need. 2: Envy.

First thing to say about Gertrude is that she's a bad mother, just as the first thing to say about Volumnia is that she's a good one. I'll amend that 'bad' to thoughtless; a less harsh judgement on a woman who can't be bothered to put herself in her son's shoes after the sudden death of his father. She sees him wearing black, silent, sad, and simply tells him to get over it: *'Thou know'st 'tis common'*, she tells him, *' – all that lives must die, / Passing through nature to eternity.' 'Ay, madam, it is common'* is his correct reply. Note that distancing 'madam'; 'mother' would have the same number of feet. Note 'common' too, and how it implies something uncommon. He has smelled a rat. Still not picking up on his disturbance, she presses him further:

If it be / Why seems it so particular with thee?

Why? Why! Is she pretending to be disingenuous because we're in public here, or is she a person whose radar is not very efficient? I think the latter; she seems to betray a slow uptake on most things. Clearly she is innocent of any hanky-panky, but still that is a pretty dim reply to a grieving son. (I mean, the old king died a most uncommon death, screaming himself to death while having a siesta.) He too knows nothing at this point:

Seems, madam? Nay, it is. I know not 'seems'.

'What you see is true, I'm not pretending'. He calls her *'good mother'* as if to get her onside, or is it to point up her badness? – and with his turmoil held in control he tells of a grief as genuine as any flamboyant suit of mourning is false. The final couplet reveals all:

...I have that within which passeth show
These but the trappings and the suits of woe.

Her silence to this confession must, I think, imply that she's been offered food for thought. She perhaps drifts back towards Claudius, unsure now, eyes on her son.

Guilty Claudius, on the other hand, picks up his nephew's signals in a trice and promptly proceeds to put Hamlet under virtual house arrest the better to keep an eye on him. This suited our South African production very well, where such edicts were once not uncommon. I could progress the course of the play with a Hamlet in his so-called madness dressed in Robben Island khaki shirt and shorts, camping out in the lobby at Elsinore with a prisoner's tin mug and plate, a rough blanket on the floor as his bed, a prison-issue Bible to hand. Words, words, words. Always on show as a prisoner of the state, and more than happy to drive Claudius nuts with anger.

Gertrude swims along in her husband's wake just as Juliet's mum does, who takes the cake for blind obedience; they both prefer to ingratiate a husband rather than comfort a child. Volumnia happily has no husband and is thus free to use her brain, which is considerable. But since mothers as a breed are so scarce in Shakespeare's canon I suppose one should be grateful that they appear at all in the plays.

(Oh, and Volumnia is a good mother because she understands the nature of her son, and takes great trouble to try to reason with him when he is in danger of making foolish judgements. I say this because I have one myself and know perfectly well that you can't make a child be what he isn't. Happily my son has no ambitions to a warrior life.)

I think Ophelia, silent, is present in this court scene, (I.ii) in a corner watching. Watching her brother's excitement at his imminent gap year, watching her lover

Hamlet, troubled, dressed in mourning. Keeping quiet as a mouse so as not to be noticed having learned that court life is safer that way. She is not mentioned as a presence onstage in the various quartos and folios in this scene however; this is just me watching out for keeping presences alive in a production.

Gertrude, not picking up on the threat implied by Claudius' ASBO urges her son to stay. He'll stay because she, his mother, has asked him to. In actual fact he has little choice. These small encounters between mother and son are important because the play is fuelled from the outset by his anger at her *'o'er hasty marriage'*. His mother matters to him. If she didn't matter to him, then his pain at her new alliance would only serve to point up the bad form of her hasty marriage rather than the hurt it engenders. The closeness of their brief initial encounter is underlined by the tone of Claudius' terse order, to regain control: *'Madam, come.'* Gertrude is not at his side and he wants her there. She goes to him of course, but her dilemma is visible; husband or son?

Act I.iii and a blithe young Ophelia takes her adored brother Laertes' warning about young men's *'primy natures'* in good spirits. Blithe? Hamlet's wooing has quite obviously elated her, hence her brother's admonitions to be a good girl and not go the whole way. There will always be a discussion in the rehearsal room about whether Hamlet and Ophelia are actually lovers. Ophelia can be seen as a shy overprotected little creature, but in our world, where girls have made huge advances in self-confidence it's surely more surprising to have a mad scene not prefigured by an initial frailty? Surprising to the audience as much as to the denizens of Elsinore. A hot-blooded adolescent struggling to cope with her first love, barely consenting to obey her father is surely more interesting to explore?

I do not know, my lord, what I should think

is not just a muddled reply to her father's prying questions, but more a sullen teenager refusing to give secrets away. She is at the last defeated by the coldness of distant grown-ups in her young life, missing her brother, wracked with loneliness, abused by her lover, tipped over the edge by her father's murder at his hands, a funeral borne by her alone. But her breakage comes not without a struggle. In another age, another clime, she would be doing drugs to ease the pain, and going mad that way.

The tumbling affection between brother and sister when the family waves goodbye to their young man must last us through the play until Laertes returns to avenge his father's death. That's from Act I to Act IV scene vii. Once Laertes has gone she is entirely at the mercy of her father's strict regime; no fraternal haven. Adolescence in young girls is a ropy time, and Polonius is a novice; good with advice, rotten with love. His spies tell him Hamlet is after Ophelia;

she is telling her father as little as possible. Judging by the 'Nunnery' scene, their relationship is very serious. Judging by Hamlet's heated confession at Ophelia's graveside, he really did love her. Hamlet does not lie. He dissembles, he plays, but he's not a liar. So I take this to be a proper love affair, or certainly the passionate precursor to one whose feelings are expressed in letters that would somersault any young girl's heart. If Hamlet had felt nothing much for Ophelia, the Nunnery scene would not be so violent. He has a dread task to fulfil, and cannot bear the burden of more than the main. He needs to show her he's truly mad in order to scare her off. That way, he hopes, his path is clear to avenge his father.

Act II.i: Hamlet comes, as she tells her father, into her room, a seemingly demented creature oddly dishevelled, and then, as if to burn her image on his retina he takes leave of her as silent as he came. Scary? Oh, yes. That's his ploy of feigning madness to avoid the pain of a sober leave-taking. But beneath the show of lunacy was he hurting? Yes, that's how it reads, positively smarting from his letters returned. Why does she obey her father about returning his love-letters? He's all she has, so how can she not obey him? Hamlet gets the idea of how to proceed with her from her rejected letters. Be cruel to be kind is Hamlet's way. However, for both of them, the muddle and hurt of breaking up so cruelly is unmistakable. But whereas Hamlet has things to do, even if he doesn't do them, she has nothing. I've said elsewhere that the trouble women have, in drama as in life, is so much to do with having nothing to occupy their minds. Sit and cry, wander far off in a garden, don't dare write to your brother because father reads your letters; choice is limited. No help from the only other woman in the joint. Ophelia too, is under a kind of house-arrest. What's to do?

And 'what's to do?' thinks Gertrude as well. That weirdness, Hamlet's *antic disposition* has panicked everyone. Big idea! Call his childhood friends to discover what's going on. Rosencrantz and Guildenstern, ready for some pocket-money, duly arrive. In Act II.ii I decided to give half of Claudius' speech to Gertrude so she could be more proactive in the scene. She interrupts Claudius with:

> *If it will please you*
> *To show us so much gentry and goodwill*
> *As to expend your time with us awhile,*
> *For the supply and profit of our hope,*
> *Your visitation shall receive such thanks*
> *As fits a king's remembrance.*

This last promissory bribe on her husband's behalf will either annoy Claudius or amuse him greatly. We get a taste of her mindset, as she shows the visiting spies out, on Guildenstern's hopeful wish that –

> *Heavens make our presence and our practises*
> *Pleasant and helpful to him.*

> *Ay, amen!*

answers Gertrude in a burst of maternal worry. And when she returns a few moments later, we go deeper into her head. Claudius says '*He tells me* [he being Polonius] *my sweet queen, he hath found / The head and source of all your son's distemper*'. She says this:

> *I doubt it is no other but the main,*
> *His father's death and our oe'rhasty marriage.*

So she can't be as dim as one had thought; a twinge of conscience peeks through. Guilt has entered her lusty soul about a son's displeasure. This is the first moment in playing Gertrude that the actor can take a bead on the woman's nature.

That elusive son's rather clunking poems of passion to Ophelia interest her, however. When Polonius reads them out, either she's appalled at her son's lack of poetic talent, or pleased the young man's fancy has turned to love, a welcome echo of her own lusty predilections:

> *Came this from Hamlet to her?*

can be read either way. Basically this is a woman in a muddle, a woman who has never properly known her son, nervous of what he'll do next, very aware now of her own indiscretion. And hey presto! – the next moment he appears, looking suitably weird (ours, as I say, was in prison garb):

Look where sadly the poor wretch comes reading

is all she can manage, and leaves at the double. Not one to either comfort or confront her own flesh and blood.

When next we see the king and queen, Claudius gives a disturbing description of the extremity of Hamlet's 'madness':

And can you by no drift of circumstance
Get from him why he puts on this confusion,
Grating so harshly all his days of quiet
With turbulent and dangerous lunacy?

Harsh, turbulent, dangerous. Strong words. Obviously the palace has been in an uproar. It's a description that should encourage bouts of extreme behaviour from the actor playing Hamlet. When they appeared, just prior to this speech of Claudius', I had our Hamlet, a wonderfully thoughtful actor called Vaneshran Arumugam, rush at the royal couple like a demented chimp and climb the wall behind them, yattering and chattering and baring his teeth. And then exit. Shock, horror, from royal party. Eyes on stalks. That *'...And...'* that begins the speech broke a frozen silence. It's a play that leaves room for any amount of invention.

The spies having arrived at Elsinore, she instructs them in being double agents, acquiesces to Claudius' plan to send poor Ophelia as bait to catch Hamlet, mouths a wish to Ophelia that her beauty and goodness will persuade him back to sanity, and departs – to her mysterious nothingness. Still hidden from us. Still open to underhand ploys. Still under Claudius' thumb. A mother without any moral muscle. An automaton. Hoping against hope that things will go away. But you can't help feeling her heart is warm though her flesh is weak. In the play scene Gertrude has one sad little line:

Come hither my dear Hamlet, sit by me.

But what young man wants to sit by his mother when there's *'metal more attractive'*?

A good sign to a hopeful mother. But now it's brave little Ophelia's turn to cope with a fiercely combative prince who proceeds to humiliate her with crass remarks, teases her in public, and yet she somehow preserves her dignity throughout. He remarks on his mother's cheerful looks, *'and my father died within's two hours'*, and when chided that twice two months have passed since he died, he responds with crushing irony: *'Then there's hope a great man's memory may outlive his life half a year.'* How do you cope with that razor-sharp mind?

No one dives in to save her; not the queen who seems preoccupied, not her father nostalging at length on the players and the play – she is abandoned to her own devices here too, poor kid. She attempts a guarded conversation with Hamlet once more but his bawdy ripostes set her back again:

> *Is this a prologue, or the posy of a ring?*
> *'Tis brief, my lord.*
> *As woman's love.*

To be blamed when it's nothing to do with you!..to be once more humiliated with bawdy remarks. She is silent. What's to say?–Gertrude's most famous line is coming up:

> *Madam, how like you this play?*
> *The lady doth protest too much, methinks.*

Hmmm…This is what she has just heard from the Player Queen:

> *In second husband let me be accurst!*
> *None wed the second but who kill'd the first.*

'Wormwood, wormwood' growls Hamlet, expressing the bitter taste in his mouth and his mind. The Player Queen goes on:

> *The instances that second marriage move*
> *Are base respects of thrift, but none of love.*
> *A second time I kill my husband dead*
> *When second husband kisses me in bed.*

And then this:

> *Both here and hence pursue me lasting strife*
> *If, once a widow, ever I be wife!*

Some awareness has to be unfurling in that slow mind of hers, some awareness of a wrongdoing. But it's too extreme to take on board. She pushes it away, such is her nature.

But then, just after Lucianus the murder-actor pours pretend poison into the ear of the sleeping king-actor and Hamlet has offered an explication, thus:

> *You shall see anon how the murderer gets the love*
> *of Gonzago's wife.*

Ophelia cries:

> *The King rises*

Gertrude, one step behind as usual:

> *How fares my lord?*

And he strides out causing great pandemonium, followed at a nervy jog by the queen while the courtiers melt away in a flapdoodle. Panicked Ophelia. Puzzled Gertrude. Triumphant Hamlet and Horatio.

Next, Claudius is given a monumentally revealing soliloquy, and we are presented with a hugely complex individual who both loves and murders and yet has a conscience. He tries to pray. Hamlet, passing by on the way to his outraged mother, declines to kill him while his soul is in touch with heaven, and proceeds on his way to mother to tell all. Gertrude the invisible, the ignorant, the gullible. Why gullible? The previous king died so suddenly. She must have been having an affair with Claudius prior to that death, must have felt a guilty pleasure that the old king was out of the way, so quick was their marriage after his funeral. She must be weighty with a great pile of guilts, made heavy with them. That second marriage meant the throne is thereby stolen from under her son's nose. No sign of her standing up for her son's inheritance. Why not? Sexual enthrallment? The old king was, well, old – Claudius younger, attentive, virile, ambitious. Altogether more fun. Claudius' accession was clearly in her interest. Little wonder that her progress towards enlightenment in the play is fitful – she appears unwilling to be enlightened.

But here follows one of the most exciting revelation scenes in all drama, the Closet Scene as it's known. In her own enseamèd bedroom, the very place where a parent's sexual excesses should not be contemplated by a child, the truth blurts itself out with a bang. Or rather a stab. Blood, death, end of Polonius behind the arras, spying yet again. It takes, though, a torrent of words from Hamlet to get Gertrude to cry out:

> *O Hamlet, speak no more*
> *Thou turn'st mine eyes into my very soul*
> *And there I see such black and grained spots*
> *As will not leave their tinct.*

The returning ghost of his father espies amazement on Gertrude's face, and that I think must be a trustworthy clue to her state of mind. Dim, defensive, in love or lust, whatever, and only half-comprehending her awful predicament. So, amazement, yes.

A son who seems to see his father's ghost, is surely a mind unhinged? But, no, very very sane:

> *Mother, for love of grace*
> *Lay not that flattering unction to your soul*
> *That not your trespass but my madness speaks.*

Only now does she fully understand how deep this goes:

> *O Hamlet, thou hast cleft my heart in twain.*

Then, from Hamlet this injunction:

> *But go not to my uncle's bed.*
> *Assume a virtue if you have it not.*

And the son goes on to instruct the mother in sexual abstinence, and to realise as well that he, too, is now a murderer. Perhaps she is weeping quietly, else why would he turn to her with such care to explain his harsh words to this stricken mother of his?

> *I must be cruel only to be kind:*

She can't think straight: *'What shall I do?'*, she begs. Head or heels, world upside down, no more love, no comfort, no haven anymore. He has already compared pictures of his murdered father and of Claudius side by side, and now, with no holds barred, he depicts her repellent lover as he sees him:

> *Not this by no means, that I bid you do:*
> *Let the bloat king tempt you again to bed,*

Pinch wanton on your cheek, call you his mouse,
And let him, for a pair of reachy kisses,
Or paddling in your neck with his damn'd fingers,
Make you ravel all the matter out,
That I essentially am not in madness,
But mad in craft. 'Twere good you let him know.

Bloat, wanton, reachy, paddling, damn'd. As if his frankness has released the last doubt in her, she speaks from her heart for the first time; an honest promise of love and loyalty to her son:

Be thou assur'd, if words be made of breath
And breath of life, I have no life to breathe
What thou hast said to me.

I feel a tangible change in the air between them in the slight pause that follows that half-line. Almost an expiration of Hamlet's breath, as if a weight has lifted. She has made a choice. Blood will out. He says in a conversational tone that was impossible before, as if to a new friend:

I must to England, you know that?

One of Shakespeare's heart-stoppingly naturalistic lines, which always take one so unawares. Gertrude is on his side at long last. Hamlet can tell her how the spies she hired will take him to England and dispose of him there. Another thing for her to absorb.

He goes, lugging Polonius out, and she's left with a horror that can only ease itself with deep sighs, *'profound heaves'* is what Claudius hears as he enters. No betrayals though, she plays up Hamlet's *'madness'* as if to the manner born; lying is now her protective shield too.

She tries, she tries hard, with no wavering from her vow; we see her slipping and sliding away from Claudius, unable to let him near her ever again. *'Come Gertrude,'* he says. She doesn't move. *'O come away!,'* he repeats. She leaves without him. *'My soul is full of discord and dismay,'* says Claudius and does not follow her. Things have changed between them.

So now Gertrude becomes a person one can start to like even. The performance I remember vividly, the one that helped me understand the woman, was Geraldine McEwen's in a Georgian production at Riverside many years ago, huge eyes wider and wider with horror as her life was revealed to her. For an actress with such an incisive intelligence she managed to seem slightly out of her depth, as if Gertrude is doing doggy-paddle from the start. Alan Rickman as Hamlet. I shamelessly stole an idea from this production for mine; after the closet scene, the haunting sound of McEwen's slippered feet slurping over the stone corridors of Elsinore, driven to insomnia, riven by guilt, wandering the palace till dawn breaks. I placed our interval after Claudius' *'Do it, England'* speech. A long first half I know, but break the action at your peril. I began the second half with the lone figure of Gertrude, in a dressing-gown, restless, smoking in the moonlight. I wanted to hold on to her story a little longer before she disappears again for ages, as Ophelia has. Hamlet and his mother are the only two people in the play who have a precious moment of real contact. Well, no, actually Hamlet and Horatio have a precious friendship. Horatio is always there when he's wanted.

We are at Act IV scene v and a fragile little girl, bereft of her father, a father killed by her lover, killed for spying, has to show us all her private agony. The two mad scenes are difficult and often infuriatingly prey to feyness or little-girliness or punk-savagery – and bad songs. (Must have been a fantastic boy who originally played this part for Shakespeare.) I can't gloss them here, they are to be so, so carefully plotted yet seem improvised. I here advocate one heart-rending instant of seeming to recognise Laertes and then – puff! – the moment has gone. Probably the less 'mad' these scenes are played, the better. I have never seen them without being nervous of my belief factor.

When Ophelia is introduced as mad, the queen is thrown. Why does she want to avoid seeing the girl? She's jumpy, nerves frayed, insomniac. Goes for long walks; why else does she know the names of all the wildflowers that grow along the bank where Ophelia drowns? She has a dense little four-line confession to the audience as

Ophelia is being fetched, describing her state of mind: the confession of a *'sick soul'*. It's too dense to understand well, but it does the trick. It's Gertrude's sole soliloquy, we must be grateful for it in a play so full of them.

Is Ophelia's first line mad or sane?

Where is the beauteous majesty of Denmark?

Has she seen a woman standing there whose beauty is ravaged and so she doesn't recognise her? Or is she way past all recognisings? Does this tell us something of the toll taken on Gertrude since she has known the truth? I feel the queen is little able to cope with such a personal disaster as Ophelia's madness; when you have your own suffering it can become too much to cope with another's. She offers a detached line here and there, but is not able to offer more. Claudius' on the other hand has become almost human, and longing to talk to his queen but she must concentrate her powers on not being touched by him. To one whose life depended on physical warmth it's hard. 'Who is this man? I don't know him anymore. He's a killer. How dangerous is he? Will he kill my son now?'

When Laertes storms in ready to attack Claudius, she holds on to the young man to calm his anger, so strongly that Claudius has to command her to let him go, not once but twice. Less, I think, to protect her husband than to defend her son, understanding perhaps that her son feels the same fury about a murdered father.

Where is my father?

     Dead   says Claudius.

       But not by him adds Gertrude.

Strange. She interrupts to differentiate the murderer in this case, seeming to want accuracy. She has ready in her mind a defensive story of Hamlet's madness, the same one she tells Claudius when he comes to her chamber, that he's *'Mad as the sea and wind'*, and therefore cannot be held responsible for any death. But she says not a single word more after this intervention, even when Ophelia reappears for her next mad scene and her brother weeps for her. Claudius, with great aplomb, manages to calm Laertes' fury, and they leave together to plot and plan, forgetting her presence. She leaves alone. Ignored. That's her new life now. There seems an answering frailty in Gertrude which Ophelia's mad scenes point up.

There is another place in the play where I found that a female presence could easily be ignored and that comes after Claudius and Polonius emerge from hiding after the 'Nunnery scene'. Ophelia's sad sonnet (*'Oh what a noble mind is here o'erthrown!'*) is usually placed as soon as he exits, forcing the two eavesdroppers to wait till it's over. But I moved it, and had the two men emerge to conduct their conversation without reference to her, practically stepping over the shaken girl, until her father, sixteen lines later seems to notice her almost accidentally with:

> *How now Ophelia*
> *You need not tell us what Lord Hamlet said*
> *We heard it all.*

She is merely a puppet in their game, and on they chatter for another ten lines before leaving after:

> *Madness in great ones must not unwatched go.*

Once they'd gone, that's where I placed her soliloquy, and it works a treat, allowing Ophelia the dignity of solitude and expansion, and a glimpse of madness lurking in the far corner of her sight:

> *O woe is me!*
> *T'have seen what I have seen, see what I see.*

I expect forgotten Gertrude goes for one of her long walks, because she next appears as an accessory to a suicide, interrupting Claudius' conference about poisoning Hamlet to tell Laertes, in forensic detail, of his sister's death. I have said I thought envy might be informing the way she silently watched and waited – *'as one incapable of her own distress'* – for the young girl to sink. A possible way out for her too? The death she describes is almost languorous, gentle, full of grace and song, an end devoutly to be wished. It seems not to occur to her to save the girl, or run for help; no, this is the right end for a wronged girl. Gertrude's mind, if it works at all, is working irresponsibly, but possibly charitably.

This is a play that baubles and bangles with deaths of all kinds, queries whether life is for living or for dying, whether revenge is sweet or sour, or can be taken at all. Whatever, death is certainly sounding in Gertrude's mind, her detached repetition of *'Drowned, drowned'* is a bell tolling more than a lament. Perhaps she envies Ophelia's relief from the pain of life that she would fain know herself. I know I'm talking like a post-Freudian here, and searching for subtexts which don't exist and probably don't matter very much, but time can crawl on a stage when you are not sure what you might be feeling or thinking. The actor's task is made harder keeping emotions alive when there's precious nothing to say, so it's an exercise we players must indulge in.

The royal exit from this scene should also tell us of the ongoing struggle she has to fight her almost Pavlovian willingness to obey a king's command. Laertes leaves, his anger at his sister's death drowning in tears. *'Let's follow Gertrude!'* he orders and berates her for her ill-timed report of Ophelia's death just when Laertes had been calmed. Then again: *'Therefore let's follow'*. Twice must mean she's not following. Perhaps by the time he's turned back to bark at her, she's gone.

So now Ophelia is no more. Now it's her pauper's burial and a darling speech of perfect grace from the queen, though she's done nothing to help the poor child to a happy marriage with her son, nor to a better burial than this one. Her Hamlet appears, returned alive from England, but ranting. His vehement declaration of love for Ophelia over the grave, no, in the grave; his violent tussle with Laertes – make her cling to the 'he's mad' story, hoping to protect him, yet hoping he's not. Mad. This woman is a lost soul. Peripheral to all the events of the play, wandering aimlessly, filling the time to come with – nothing. Low energy creature, entirely living at another's bidding. A wraith. Bereft even of a daughter now.

Back to Elsinore and the final fight. She has one thing to do while a thought curls up in her skull biding its time, which is to make amends, be a peacemaker, tie up string-ends the way one wants to do when no time is left. She makes Hamlet and Laertes shake hands before they fight. She is all for her son now, ready to mop his brow, watchful of Claudius and I think probably noticing everything closely. Picks up a cup to drink to her son's health, and Claudius practically shouts at her not to drink. In that moment she knows everything. His voice gives it all away, as clear as daylight.

Gertrude! Do not drink!

I will, my lord; I pray you pardon me.

There's an odd stage direction in the Arden Edition though it has the grace to appear in brackets. It says: *She drinks [and offers the cup to Hamlet]*. Er, no, guys, she does not. She has seen her murderer husband popping a pearl into the goblet, and I believe that she has overheard her husband hiss to Laertes at the end of the burial scene, this give-away:

> *Strengthen your patience in our last night's speech:*
> *We'll put the matter to the present push.*
> *Good Gertrude, set some watch over your son.*

He seems to notice her proximity a touch too late, and has to think quickly. If she's to be given an ounce of respect at the end of it all, then Gertrude has got to put two and two together and be resolved that she will bloody well keep some watch over her son herself. Else what is the woman doing? Just hanging around waiting for an exit? Picking a daisy to put on Ophelia's corpse?) So, back to the drink:

> *I will my lord; I pray you pardon me.*

Insurrection at last. And freedom! This is a mini-Hedda speaking here! She just cannot drink *innocently* at this point, it would take from the queen the very last vestige of moral intelligence if she did. No, she must know what she's doing and she must want it by now, her life is so pointless. She must drink to warn Hamlet there's villainy abroad. So she drinks it all down, she wants to wipe the sweat off her son's brow, get close, be a mother, but he's busy fencing. Eleven lines and a huge fight later, she falls and only Osric notices.

Another four lines and though her son is wounded, bleeding, he notices his fallen mother. The king lies to the company; says she just swooned at the sight of blood.

No, no! the drink, the drink! O my dear Hamlet!
The drink, the drink! I am poison'd.

That's emphatic enough for anyone trying to get a message across, isn't it? That's all the information he needs. I always want her to die *after* Hamlet's next line, not before. I want her to hear her son taking a clear lead over events. No one will ever notice when exactly poor Gertrude's soul leaves her body, but she will die a better death having tried her utmost to save her son. I've not played the part, and never will, but I'd guess that's worth working for over a long evening.

There's a miraculous painting by Breughel called *The Fall of Icarus*: a farmer ploughs his land on a cliff-top in the foreground and far away to the right a small figure losing his wing-feathers is plunging head first into the sea below. The great event goes almost unnoticed. What I have tried to describe is the reverse of that. The humble ploughman drowns and shining Icarus holds the foreground gaze.

Epilogue

S O THERE WE are – our self-respect a tad traduced still by the general airy acceptance that boys – not grown men even, but mere boys – quite acceptably acted parts which even today rise head and shoulders above anything written since for exquisite combinings of wit, romance, daring, courage, and fatal love. Dammit.

Even he who wrote these characters has to be elevated out of his humble beginnings and thrown into a class from whom one has not particularly noted the heart nor the humanity for which he is specially noted. For that alone I'd keep him lowly, thank you, with a mind quite untrammelled by ideas received from a tertiary education if for no more reason than to keep solidarity with his modest, uneducated but very human sisters worldwide. For the rest he's a genius and out of all classes therefore.

And then just look at these parts which count among the best available, apart from the few I write about in this little book: Masha and Millamant, Bracknell and Beatrice – Ranevskaya, Helena, Nora, Electra, and lots more. Not one of them, however, has a nature free of being what it is except by virtue of loving someone who they should either marry or walk away from. Oh well, OK, Electra, but she needs her brother to do what she wants done. None of them can climb a throne, defeat an enemy, or pronounce a thought which isn't about love or its appurtenances. Oh well, alright, Antigone.

Thus it's a limited field. Even if we forget a one-off like *Hamlet* for a moment, there's still no chance for us of a Titus, a Lear, in fact any old king – someone who takes the stage because of his nature and position not his marital status, a person with autonomy, endowed with ambition or madness enough to cleave some path. Lady Macbeth who has ambition in spades loses her mettle, falls into weak-headed lunacy, and then simply dwindles away. One understands the writer keeping his eye on the main man, but you get the point. Even Shakespeare's generous pen couldn't manage a resolution where a woman sees her villainy through to her bitter end. Malfi achieves her death in magnificent poetry, though she is killed off betimes; the play rambles on after its uniquely eponymous heroine is gone for too long. Margaret of Anjou, once a force on a battlefield, up to slapping her enemy across the face with a napkin still wet with his own son's life-blood, is reduced to a super-nag in her dotage. Not for her any musings on the metaphysics of her life, just a barrage of curses. Cleopatra alone has the dignity of philosophising for a short while as she paces the prison of her monument. Her speech beginning:

My desolation does begin to make a better life… et seq is the nearest a woman in drama gets to a profound rumination on her fall from grace. Hers is not an extravagant treat, mind you, fairly cursory compared with thoughtful Richard's; her crown proves hollower than his. Or is it that sustained thought from a woman is just not sexy?

Think of Mary Ure ironing Jimmy Porter's shirts while he lets off reams of verbal steam. Think of Vivien Merchant's silk-clad legs suggestively crossing themselves, with nothing more to offer a room full of randy old men than that silent provocation. Rattigan's and Williams' women are dream-women who are really men; frilly dreams of frailty and fear. Oh, alright, Albee's feisty Martha. Coward's women are of their time, Wilde's irresistibly funny, but stuck there too.

So be it. Way to go. Women must continue to enter the marketplace, earn their powerful positions, express themselves articulately, and hang on for dear life to the swinging self-confidence that young girls today possess before they succumb to expectations and then 'dwindle into wives'.

Things might change, but for now, the mirror held up to nature frustrates, and any full-blooded actress not content with her cleavage alone will surely concur.

End of Krapette's Last Tape.

Bibliography

Bellow, Saul (1988), *Saul Bellow's Herzog*, ed. by Harold Bloom. New York: Chelsea House

Bernard Shaw, George (1922), *The Quintessence of Ibsenism*. London: Constable & Co.

Bernard Shaw, George (1924), *St Joan*. London: Penguin Plays

Brook, Peter (2012), 'Alas Poor Yorick' in *The Quality of Mercy*. London: Nick Hern Books

Chambers, Colin (1988), *Blackwell Companion to Twentieth Century Theatre*. Oxford: Blackwell Publishing

Durbach, Errol (1980) (ed.), *Ibsen and the Theatre: Essays in Celebration of the 150th Anniversary of Ibsen's Birth*. London: Macmillan

Greer, Germaine (2009), *Shakespeare's Wife*. London: Harper Perennial

Greer, Germaine (1986), *Shakespeare: A Very Short Introduction*. Oxford: Oxford University Press

Hill, Holly (1987), *Playing Joan: Actresses on the Challenge of Shaw's Saint Joan: Twenty-Six Interviews*. New York: Theatre Communications Group

Ibsen, Henrik (1967), *Hedda Gabler*, trans. by Michael Meyer. London: Methuen & Co Ltd

Johnson, Ben (1953), *Ben Jonson's Timber or Discoveries,* ed. by Ralph S Walker. New York: Syracuse University Press

Nicholl, Charles (2007), *The Lodger: Shakespeare on Silver Street*. London: Allen Lane

Pitt, Angela (1981), *Shakespeare's Women*. Devon: David & Charles

Shakespeare, William (2001), *Antony & Cleopatra: The Applause Shakespeare Library*, ed. by Barry Gaines, theatre commentary by Janet Suzman. New York; London: Applause

Shakespeare, William (2003), *Hamlet,* ed. by Harold Jenkins. London: Thomson Learning, first pub. 1982 by The Arden Shakespeare/Methuen.

Sitwell, Edith (1965), *A Notebook on William Shakespeare*. London: Macmillan & Co.

Wade, Laura (2010), *Posh*. London: Oberon Books

Wilson, John Dover (1932), *The Essential Shakespeare*. Cambridge: Cambridge University Press

References to other work

Anonymous, dir. by Roland Emmerich, screenplay by John Orloff (Columbia Pictures, 2011)

Shakespeare in Love, dir. by John Madden, screenplay by Tom Stoppard and Marc Norman (Miramax Lionsgate, 1999)

The Gospel According to Saint Matthew, dir. by Pier Paolo Pasolini (Legend Films Inc., 1964)

The Fall of Icarus, Pieter Breughel, oil on canvas, mounted on wood (c. 1558)

Janet Suzman was born in Johannesburg, graduated from the University of Witwatersrand, trained at LAMDA, and joined the RSC for its inaugural season, *The Wars of the Roses* in 1962, where she stayed on and off for a decade playing many of the heroines and culminating in a memorable Cleopatra. She is an Hon. Associate Artist of that company. She has since pursued a richly varied career in all manner of performance disciplines; among them *The Singing Detective* and *The Draughstman's Contract* on TV and Fellini's *The Boat Sails On* on film. She has twice won *The Evening Standard* Best Actress Award (Chekhov and Fugard), had Academy Award and Golden Globe nominations (*Nicholas and Alexandra*), twice won The Liverpool Echo Best Production Award (Miller and Shakespeare), and also the TMA Best Production for her *Cherry Orchard* transposed to contemporary South Africa aka *The Free State*. *The Johannesburg Othello* – so named by Channel Four TV and aired in 1988 – was her directorial debut for The Market Theatre of which she is a founding Patron. She was awarded the Pragnell Shakespeare Prize in 2012 and is an Honorary Fellow of the Shakespeare Trust, University of Birmingham. She was appointed DBE for services to drama in 2011.